The ESSEN

CW00968145

FORTRAN

Rev. Dennis C. Smolarski, S.J., Ph.D.
Assistant Professor of Mathematics
Santa Clara University, California

Research and Education Association
61 Ethel Road West
Piscataway, New Jersey 08854

THE ESSENTIALS® OF FORTRAN I

Printed in the United States of America

Library of Congress Catalog Card Number 89-60901

International Standard Book Number 0–87891–663-6

Revised Printing, 1992

ESSENTIALS is a registered trademark of
Research and Education Association, Piscataway, New Jersey

WHAT "THE ESSENTIALS" WILL DO FOR YOU

This book is a review and study guide. It is comprehensive and it is concise.

It helps in preparing for exams, in doing homework, and remains a handy reference source at all times.

It condenses the vast amount of detail characteristic of the subject matter and summarizes the **essentials** of the field.

It will thus save hours of study and preparation time.

The book provides quick access to the important facts, principles, theorems, concepts, and equations in the field.

Materials needed for exams can be reviewed in summary form – eliminating the need to read and re-read many pages of textbook and class notes. The summaries will even tend to bring detail to mind that had been previously read or noted.

This "ESSENTIALS" book has been prepared by an expert in the field, and has been carefully reviewed to assure accuracy and maximum usefulness.

Dr. Max Fogiel
Program Director

CONTENTS

CHAPTER 1

BACKGROUND AND INTRODUCTION

1.1 HISTORY

FORTRAN is an acronym for FORmula TRANslation. This scientific computer language was developed in the early 1950's by John W. Backus of the International Business Machine Corporation (IBM) in San Jose, California, as an easier-to-use alternate to programming in what is now called "Assembly Language." Since its original definition in 1955, FORTRAN has gone through a number of revisions, and today there exist several dialects and versions of FORTRAN.

The major dialects in common use are called FORTRAN IV and FORTRAN 77. FORTRAN IV appeared in the late 1960's and is also called FORTRAN-66 (the '66' refers to 1966, the year of development). In the late 1970's, the FORTRAN standards committee approved a new version of FORTRAN, called FOR-TRAN-77. Work is also progressing on another revision of FORTRAN which, although not yet approved, is sometimes referred to as FORTRAN-88.

1.2 STATEMENT TYPES AND FORMAT

New versions of FORTRAN have been so written, that older

1

programs do not (in general) have to be revised. All versions of FORTRAN also follow conventions established in the early 1950's when all input to computers was via Hollerith (so-called "IBM" or "computer punch") cards.

As a result, the following rules apply to all versions of FORTRAN.

1. There are four types of "lines" (or "cards" if one thinks in terms of entering information via computer cards).

   a. Initial (Statement) lines

   b. Continuation lines

   c. Comment lines

   d. END lines

"Cards" and "lines" will be used interchangeably hereafter.

2. Each line has 80 columns and lines not used for comments subdivided into four subsections or fields.

   a. Columns 1-5 are reserved for the numeric statement label (vaguely corresponding to the BASIC line number, although each FORTRAN line does *not* have to have a label). For most lines, this field is left blank. If a statement label is needed, any integer number (from 1 to 5 digits) may be placed anywhere in the field – no distinction is made between right and left justification.

   b. Column 6 is used to indicate whether a line is a continuation of the previous line. For most lines, this field is also left blank. Any non-blank character in column 6 will turn

2

a line into such a "continuation line."

c. Columns 7 - 72 are used for any valid FORTRAN statement. Except in literal quotation strings, all blanks are ignored in this field when the information is interpreted by the compiler. (Blanks do take up one of the allowable columns, however.) Although FORTRAN statements cannot start before column 7, it is permitted to start such statements after column 7.

d. Columns 73 - 80 were/are used for printing/punching a machine generated line identification number (or sometimes a programmer chosen job number). Since the number in this field was an identification number rather than a programming instruction, even in FORTRAN-77, any information which a programmer might put in this field is ignored! Thus, even though something may appear on a line past column 73, it is ignored by the compiler (and thus can be a source of errors)!

3. If the letter C is put into column 1, the entire line is considered to be a COMMENT, and is ignored by the compiler. FORTRAN-77 also allows an asterisk (*) in column 1 instead of a C. A comment line cannot come between an initial line and any continuation lines. A FORTRAN comment exists only for one line, and cannot be continued to the next line. If the text of a comment must continue over more than one line, each line must be designated as a separate comment line by the use of another C (or *) in column 1.

4. Each section of code (i.e., main program, subroutine, function), must have an END statement as the last line physically. An END statement is simply a line with the word END somewhere in columns 7-72 and blank spaces elsewhere.

5. A line which is neither a continuation line, a comment line, or an END line is called an INITIAL line and can contain any valid FORTRAN statement according to the field format mentioned in section 2c. above.

6. Some compilers will give an error or warning message if a completely blank line is encountered. Thus, if blank lines are desired to improve readability of the source code, such lines should have a C (or *) in column 1 to avoid any unnecessary error or warning messages.

7. Most FORTRAN compilers are *not* sensitive to the case of letters of the alphabet. They may be upper case or lower case – A and a are considered to be the same letter. Because the card punch machines of the 1950's did not have lower case letters, descriptions and examples in books are traditionally in upper case letters only. Even though the examples given below will use upper case letters, a programmer should remember that for most compilers, lower case letters may also be used.

1.3 PROGRAM HEADER STATEMENT AND PROGRAM SKELETON

The PROGRAM header statement is optional in FORTRAN-77 and is permitted in some dialects of FORTRAN-IV. Its sole purpose is to give a name to the main program segment. Sometimes local dialects require input/output file specifications as well.

If used, its form is:

```
7+
PROGRAM name
```

Note: Here and elsewhere, the '7+' is a reminder that what follows on the next line starts in column 7 (or later).

Compared to other popular programming languages, the FORTRAN skeleton is almost non-existent. Because there are no generally "reserved words" in FORTRAN, the skeleton is merely:

```
7+
[PROGRAM name]    {optional}
[variable type declarations] {optional}
<statements>
END
```

1.4 THE STOP STATEMENT

The last executable statement before the END is usually a STOP statement. Its format is merely

```
7+
STOP
```

The STOP statement terminates the program, in most cases returning control back to the operating system. Because of the existence of "GO TO"'s in FORTRAN, the STOP statement (which marks the logical ending point of a program), need not always come right before the END line (which marks the physical ending point of a program segment). Also, more than one STOP may be included in a program. Some dialects permit the use of CALL EXIT in lieu of a STOP, and some even allow the omission of a STOP if it would come right before the END line.

5

1.5   SAMPLE PROGRAM

```
                     Column Number
          00000000011111111112222222222333333333344444444445
          12345678901234567890123456789012345678901234567890

Line Number
1                    PROGRAM SAMP1
2            C
3            C        SAMPLE PROGRAM TO PRODUCE A LIST OF
4            C        NUMBERS AND THEIR SQUARES
5            C
6            C        VARIABLE DECLARATIONS
7            C
8                    INTEGER NUM, NUMSQR
9            C
10                   WRITE (6,*) 'NUMBER - Number-Squared'
11                   DO 231 NUM=1,10
12                      NUMSQR = NUM*NUM
13                      WRITE (6,*) NUM, NUMSQR
14        231          CONTINUE
15                   STOP
16                   END
```

Comments

Lines 1-7, 9 are comment lines. Note the C in column 1 on each line. Note that lines 2, 3, 7 and 9 are blank comment lines, inserted for readability.

Lines 11-14 form the calculation loop, which is performed 10 times. The operation of this loop is discussed in Chapter 5. Note that while line 11 and 14 start in column 7, the interior of the loop is indented for readability.

Lines 10 and 13 are WRITE statements, to convey information from the program. This is discussed in Chapters 3 and 4.

Note that line 14 contains a statement number in the initial field (columns 1-5). This statement number is referenced back in line 11 (after the keyword DO).

Note also that none of the 16 lines in the program is a "continuation" line since in each case, column 6 is left blank.

Line 15, the STOP statement, is the logical end of the program. After the completion of the loop, there is nothing more to do, so the computer is told to STOP.

Line 16, the END statement, is the physical end of this segment of the program. In longer programs, another program segment (i.e., a subprogram like a SUBROUTINE or a FUNC-TION) may follow at this point.

1.6 GOOD, BAD, AND DIFFERENCES

This is a list of the major features of FORTRAN, which may be especially useful for those who have used other languages.

Portable Code–Because of the standardization of FOR-TRAN, programs can be readily moved from one compiler to another and run, usually with only minor changes, at most.

Efficient Compilers–FORTRAN compilers are very well developed, usually with many optimization features, and are available for almost all machines, from a personal computer to a Cray. Because of this efficiency, FORTRAN programs usually run fast.

Exponentiation Operator–FORTRAN has an exponentiation operation, **, which makes it particularly useful for solving numerical problems.

Mathematical Features–Standard FORTRAN contains several features which make it very appropriate for mathematical programs: COMPLEX and DOUBLE PRECISION data types, the exponentiation operator, and a large library of built-in mathematical functions.

Powerful Input/Output–FORTRAN has a developed input/output system with many features. As a result, the input and output system is very powerful (but can also be very confusing to use).

Blanks Are Ignored–All blanks (except in literal quoted strings) are ignored. Thus FORTRAN differs from some other languages, where certain blanks are needed and only "extra" blanks and carriage returns are ignored. In FORTRAN, blanks are even ignored as part of variable names (see Chapter 2).

Identifiers Are Six Characters Long–FORTRAN variables and subprogram names can (normally) only be six characters long at most. Therefore, a programmer has to be somewhat creative in choosing appropriate identifiers.

Default Variable Typing–Variables do *not* have to be declared in FORTRAN. Variables which are not declared (possibly because of misspellings) are given a default numeric "type" (INTEGER or REAL) based on the first letter (cf. Section 2.2).

Block If In FORTRAN-77–FORTRAN-77 does have a block IF structure (IF-THEN-ELSE), which did not exist in FORTRAN IV. However, standard FORTRAN-77 still does not have a conditional loop (e.g., WHILE or REPEAT) although many major compilers include a version of the WHILE loop as a standard extension.

Variations In The Counted Loop–The counted loop (i.e., the so-called "DO"-loop) in FORTRAN IV could only count up, and had to start with a positive number, but it could have a step size. The counted loop in FORTRAN-77 can start anywhere, and be given a negative step size, allowing it to "count down."

No Recursion–FORTRAN subprograms are not recursive.

All Variables Are Local–All variables in FORTRAN are local to the subsection in which they are used and/or declared. There are no global variables in FORTRAN. The same holds true for statement numbers – they are independent by subsection.

No Reserved Word "BEGIN"–There is no reserved word BEGIN in FORTRAN, and thus there is only one END per section – physically the last line of the section.

No Semicolons–Standard FORTRAN does not use semicolons to separate statements, and only one statement can appear on a line. (Some extensions permit multiple statements, however.)

New Lines Have Meaning–Because semicolons are not part of the FORTRAN syntax, the new line (carriage return)

9

separates statements. If one line continues information from the previous line (e.g., a very long arithmetic expression), it must be indicated as a continuation line (by a non-blank character in column 6).

Spaghetti-Code Syndrome–FORTRAN can lead to a so-called "spaghetti-code" style of programming, unless the programmer uses disciplined, structured techniques. Old FORTRAN programs are often much harder to read than programs written in FORTRAN-77 or other structured languages.

CHAPTER 2

VARIABLES, CONSTANTS, AND ASSIGNMENT STATEMENTS

2.1 VARIABLE LENGTH

Variables in FORTRAN are names for memory locations. They may be used to reference simple, scalar quantities, or they may be arrays used to reference multiple memory locations (see Chapter 9).

Variable names follow the rules of any symbolic FORTRAN identifier. In FORTRAN, symbolic identifiers may be between 1 and 6 letters and numbers in length, with the first character always being a letter. (Many compilers will allow variables to have a longer length but may give a warning and/or ignore all characters other than the first 6.) Note that since all blanks are ignored (except in literal quotation strings), blanks may be included as part of variable names (but this is not recommended)! As mentioned in section 1.2, no distinction is made between upper case and lower case letters of the alphabet.

Thus, for example,

```
I,A, SAM, NUMBER
```

are all valid FORTRAN variable names,

are *not* valid identifiers. (NUMBERS is too long, 3AXES begins with a number, and A_#B contains illegal characters). Also note that on most compilers NUMTST is interpreted the same as NUM TST or N UMT S T.

2.2 DATA TYPES, DEFAULT TYPING, DECLARATIONS

Each variable (i.e., memory location) is associated with one type of information or data. FORTRAN-77 data types are INTEGER, REAL, CHARACTER, LOGICAL, COMPLEX, and DOUBLE PRECISION. (Standard FORTRAN-IV does not allow variables of type CHARACTER.) In a given subsection of a program, a variable can be associated only with one data type and that type cannot be changed in the course of that program section.

Each variable is local in FORTRAN (unlike some other popular languages), and variables do *not* have to be declared. If a variable is *not* explicitly declared before use, it is given a default *numeric* type based on the first letter. If the first letter is between I and N (inclusive), the variable is considered to refer to an INTEGER quantity. Otherwise, the variable is considered to be REAL. Thus, NUMBER would, by default typing, refer to an INTEGER number, and SAM would, by default typing, refer to a REAL number.

One may explicitly declare variables by using a TYPE statement, indicating the data type first, and then the variables of that type (separated by commas). There may be more than one declaration statement of the same type. As usual, by standard convention, the type name must start no earlier than column 7.

As an example,

```
7+
REAL A,B,C
INTEGER I,NUMBER
INTEGER PETE
LOGICAL MORE
```

This declares the variables A, B, and C to be of data type REAL, the variables I, NUMBER, and PETE to be of type INTEGER, and the variable MORE to be of type LOGICAL.

Note: Since variables do *not* have to be declared in FORTRAN, one never gets the compiler error "variable undeclared" as in some other major contemporary languages. Because of this, misspellings (and mistypings) are not automatically caught. Variables which are not declared (possibly because of misspellings) automatically receive the default numeric data type.

2.3   IMPLICIT TYPE STATEMENT

One can change the default typing of variables by using the IMPLICIT type declaration statement. For example,

```
7+
IMPLICIT INTEGER (A-N)
```

will cause all variables which begin with any letter between A and N inclusively to be automatically typed as INTEGER.

From the point of view of contemporary programming style, IMPLICIT statements (and default typing) should be avoided, and each variable should be separately declared.

13

2.4 CONSTANTS

INTEGER constants are written as whole numbers without any decimal point (or commas). REAL numbers can be either written in standard (i.e., "floating point") notation (containing a decimal point) or in scientific (i.e., exponential) notation (a number with or without a decimal point, followed by an E, followed by an integer which is the exponent of 10). INTEGER and REAL numbers may be preceded by an optional sign. Thus,

```
10 -24 134579 are integers.

3.1415926 -3.2E5 0.3456E-57 are real numbers.

-3.2E5 represents -3.2 x 10⁵
= -3.2 x 100,000 = -3,200,000.0
```

LOGICAL constants are discussed in Chapter 8. CHARACTER constants are discussed in Chapter 11. Constants for DOUBLE PRECISION and COMPLEX numbers are discussed in Chapter 12.

2.5 ARITHMETIC OPERATIONS

FORTRAN arithmetic operators include the standard four operators of addition (+), subtraction (−), multiplication (*), and division (/). FORTRAN *does* possess an exponentiation operator, indicated by two asterisks (**). Thus, "A to the power of B" is written in FORTRAN as "A**B".

The standard algebraic precedence of operations holds, so that exponentiation is performed before multiplication and division, and multiplication and division are performed before addition and subtraction.

When two or more arithmetic operators of equal precedence occur in the same expression, they are evaluated left to right (i.e., as one normally reads the expression), with the exception of two exponentiation operators next to each other. Standard convention is that A**B**C is interpreted as A**(B**C), i.e., the evaluation is done right to left.

Whenever there can be any confusion, one should always force the order of precedence by using parentheses.

2.6 NOTE ON DIVISION

In FORTRAN there is only one division operator which is used for any division between numbers of whatever data type. If BOTH operands involved are INTEGER, an integer division is performed, i.e., any fractional part is ignored. In other cases, however, the result is numerically appropriate to the two operands (whether they be REAL, DOUBLE PRECISION or COMPLEX).

Older versions of FORTRAN demanded that both operands in any arithmetic operation match in type, and this could be forced by the use of a type conversion function (cf. Chapter 6). This is no longer required, however.

The FORTRAN division rule can cause unexpected problems. Suppose that IA is declared to be of type INTEGER, and suppose IA is assigned the value of 10, then

```
IA/20
```

evaluates to zero, since the integer division of 10 by 20 is less than one and fractions are discarded. However,

```
IA/20.0
```

evaluates to 0.5 since in this case 20.0 is a real number and a real division is performed (which retains the fraction).

Thus, given that IA has the value of 10,

```
3*(IA/20)
```

evaluates to 0, but

```
3*(IA/20.0)
```

evaluates to 1.50.

2.7   ASSIGNMENT STATEMENTS

Variables are assigned new values simply by using the equals sign (=). The variable receiving a new value is placed on the left side of the equals sign. Only a single variable may be on the left side of the equals sign in an assignment statement. Thus,

```
X = 3.0*A**2 + 2.0*B - C
```

is a valid FORTRAN assignment statement.

Conversion functions exist to convert between fundamental numeric types, but FORTRAN-77 performs these conversions automatically, and, thus, the use of the conversion functions is optional.

In FORTRAN-77, if an expression is real, it can be assigned to an integer variable – the fractional portion of the number will be discarded (and thus the number is *not* rounded, but rather truncated).

16

Similarly, if an expression is integer, it can also be assigned to a real variable – it is converted automatically.

The older conversion functions (which were mandatory in certain cases in former versions of FORTRAN) may still be used, and they will be mentioned in Chapter 6. For good programming style, their use is recommended.

CHAPTER 3

INTRODUCTION TO FORMATTED INPUT/OUTPUT

3.1 OVERVIEW

In standard FORTRAN, the input/output commands have two parts to them:

a. an input/output command statement with a list of variables,

b. a FORMAT statement specifying how the variables are to be read-in/written-out.

We now look briefly at both of these parts.

3.2 INPUT/OUTPUT COMMANDS

The standard input command is:

```
READ(IDEV,IFORM) <variable list>
```

and the standard output command is:

```
WRITE(IDEV,IFORM) <variable list>
```

18

IDEV refers to the "device" number. Historically, this was required to distinguish between different input or output devices on single-user systems. IDEV may be an integer constant, or it can be an integer variable (whose value is assigned by a standard arithmetic assignment statement). Values vary from installation to installation, but often 2 refers to the card reader, 3 refers to the line printer, 5 to terminal input, and 6 to terminal output. Most systems allow the user to specify associations between "device" numbers and stored files, requiring a user to predetermine this association when writing the program (see OPEN, CLOSE commands described below in 3.9). However, some systems allow this association to be done at run or compile time.

IFORM refers to the FORMAT statement number which will be discussed in the next section and in the example below. IFORM should normally be an integer constant, but it may be an integer variable whose value (a statement label) is assigned by means of the ASSIGN statement.

The <variable list> is a list of variables separated by commas. If no variable values are needed (e.g., if a WRITE statement is to print out a constant character string), then the <variable list> may be omitted.

For example,

```
READ(5,100)  A,B,C,D
WRITE(6,101)  A,B,C
WRITE(6,102)
```

3.3   FORMAT STATEMENTS

A FORMAT statement is technically a "non-executable" statement, an important distinction for some purposes. A FOR-

MAT statement must have a statement number and takes on the following general form:

```
     7+
100  FORMAT( <descriptor list> )
```

Within the parentheses of the FORMAT statement is a list of "field descriptors" separated by commas. They are used to describe the input/output line space by space (i.e., column by column). Each FORMAT statement describes at least ONE line. Physically, FORMAT statements can be put anywhere in a program segment, however, there are two general styles:

a. near (next to) the corresponding READ/WRITE,

b. all together in a block at the beginning or end of the program segment.

Note: A FORMAT statement referenced by a READ or WRITE statement must be in the same program segment as the corresponding READ or WRITE statement – it cannot be in a separate subprogram. Thus, the same FORMAT statement label number may be re-used by statements in separate subprogram sections, since statement labels are also local in FORTRAN.

3.4   BASIC FIELD DESCRIPTORS

In general, field descriptors consist of two main parts, a letter and a number (or combination of numbers) which follows it. The letter is characteristic and corresponds to the variable's data type in the input or output statement. The number combination indicates the number of spaces set aside for input or output. The most common descriptors are the following:

In   Integer:

            n – the number of spaces needed.

In.m   Integer:

            n – the total number of spaces needed.

            m – the minimum number of digits printed.

This forces initial zeroes if the actual number has fewer than
m digits.

Fw.d   Real number in FIXED form:

            w – total number of spaces needed.

            d – number of spaces to the right of the decimal
                  point.

Ew.d   Real number in EXPONENTIAL form:

            w – total number of spaces needed.

            d – number of spaces to the right of the decimal
                  point.

An E descriptor (for output) needs space for the letter E, 3 spaces
for the exponent and its sign, the decimal point, and an initial zero
with a possible minus sign. Thus, in general (for output), *w* should
be greater than or equal to d + 7.

Ew.dEe   Real number in EXPONENTIAL form:

            w and d are same as in the previous version.

            e – the number of digits in the exponent.

In this case, *w* must be greater than or equal to d+e+5.

nX   Spacing:

            the number *n* before the *X* indicates how many blanks
            should be left (on output), or columns skipped (on
            input).

nHstring   Hollerith (named after the inventor of the "IBM"-
            card–used in OUTPUT FORMATs to output a literal

21

string of characters):
the number *n* before the H indicates how many characters follow the H.

<matched single quotes>
Alternate to the H format to output a literal string of characters. A single quote surrounds the literal string on both sides. If the string is to contain a single quote, that quote is indicated by two single quotes immediately next to each other.

Note: Most FORTRAN-IV systems allow the use of single quotes instead of requiring the H format. However, one might find a FORTRAN-IV system which still uses double quotes instead of the H descriptor and will give an error if single quotes are used.

/End of record separator:
–on OUTPUT, this will cause a "new line" (unless the new carriage control determines otherwise).

–on INPUT, this will cause the rest of the input line to be ignored and also start the reading on the next line. They can be used instead of commas, and more than one can be joined together.

Note: If the field width is too small to fit the number which is supposed to be printed, FORTRAN will not expand the field to fit the number. In this situation, many FORTRAN compilers will fill the output field with asterisks (and give a run-time error).

3.5 BRIEF EXAMPLES

I10   An integer field which can hold a maximum of 10 digits. If this is used in an OUTPUT FORMAT and a number less than 10 digits is requested, the number

will appear right-justified in the field.
E.g., bbbb136787 (where b indicates a blank space).

F10.3   A fixed real number field which can hold a number which has 6 digits before the decimal point, and 3 digits to the right of the decimal point.
E.g., bbb123.340

E10.2   A real number field in which the number is written in scientific notation. This only allows 3 digits before the decimal point and 2 afterward, since the other spaces are taken up with the decimal point and exponent. E.g., b-0.23E+03

3X   A blank field which forces 3 blank spaces (between fields).

5HHELLO A Hollerith field which could be used to print out the 5 character literal string HELLO.

'HELLO' Alternative Hollerith field which could be used to print out the literal string HELLO.

3.6 CARRIAGE CONTROL

In FORMAT statements used with WRITE commands (for OUTPUT), the first character (number, letter, symbol, or blank), which would be printed is actually not printed and is used as a "carriage control" character which determines where the rest of the line will be printed (i.e., top of next page, next available line, skip a line, overstrike). This applies to files printed on traditional line printers – if the same file appears on a terminal screen or on a personal printer, the "carriage control" characters do not affect the terminal or printer in the same way, and they are actually printed.

One way of thinking about "carriage control characters" is to imagine the first "printable" character being placed in a special (non-printing) column "0" or (Carriage Control) column "cc" which comes right before the first printable column #1.

The standard carriage control characters are:

blank   print on the next available line

1   perform a top-of-form before printing (i.e., go to the top of the next page)

0   skip a line before printing (i.e., double-space)

+   overstrike the last line

Note: the + can be used in special cases, as when one wants to underline certain words!

Local implementations frequently augment these basic carriage control characters with others, so unknown and untested "carriage control" characters should be avoided.

Usually, for FORMATs used for output, the standard practice to insure that no accidents occur (with wrong, unintended numbers/characters being put into the carriage control column) is to begin the list of field descriptors with a 1X or a 1H, or ' '.

3.7   EXAMPLES

3.7.1   SHORT EXAMPLE

```
A = 2.0
B = 5.321
```

```
        I = 126
        WRITE(6, 121) A,I,B
121     FORMAT(1X,F5.3,I5,F6.2)
        STOP
        END
```

OUTPUT:

```
column numbers ——>
cc   1 2 3 4 5 6 7 8 9 10 11 12 13 14 15 16

     2 . 0 0 0     1 2 6         5 . 3 2
```

Explanation:

The first field descriptor, 1X, forces one blank to be the initial item in the output line. Since this is the first item determined by the FORMAT, it is used as the carriage control character (or, we may just as easily consider it to be placed in "column cc".)

Columns 1-5 were set aside for the value of the variable A, by the next descriptor F5.3. Since three decimal places were requested, three decimal places were given – all zeroes, but his necessitated the decimal point going in column 2.

The next 5 columns (columns 6-10) were set aside for the value of the integer variable I. That value was printed right justified in that field, i.e., the last digit was printed in the last column (column number 10).

Then the next 6 columns (columns 11-16) were set aside for the value of the real variable B. Only two decimal places were requested, necessitating that the decimal point go in column 14. Thus, the number was rounded to two decimal places.

3.7.2 LONGER EXAMPLE

```fortran
      INTEGER I,J,K
      REAL A,B,C
      A = 123.45
      B = 6.7
      C = .89
      I = 1
      J = 234
      K = 56789
      WRITE(6,521) A,I,B,J,C,K
  521 FORMAT(1X,F10.3,I5//'0',F8.2,
     1 2X,I5//1H ,'C=',E10.3,I7)
      STOP
      END
```

```
Output

line #    -->  column number
     cc   1  2  3  4  5  6  7  8  9 10 11 12 13 14 15 16 17 18 19 20

 1                    1  2  3  .  4  5  0              1
 2
 3
 4*   0
 5                       6  .  7  0              2  3  4
 6
 7
 8
 9        C  =      0  .  8  9  0  E  +  0  0        5  6  7  8  9
```

* Line 4 – The 0 in the carriage control column indicates that the rest of the output line is actually printed on the next available line. The 0 itself never appears.

26

3.8 REPETITION FACTORS

One can also prefix the standard numeric field descriptors with a "repetition factor", a constant which "multiplies" the occurrences of the descriptor in the FORMAT. For example,

```
100   FORMAT(3I2,2F10.5)
```

is equivalent to

```
100   FORMAT(I2,I2,I2,F10.5,F10.5)
```

3.9 CHECKING FOR THE END OF THE INPUT FILE

FORTRAN-77 (and many FORTRAN IV compilers) allow a user to test to see if the input file has any more data in it. To do this, the programmer expands the control number section of the READ statement and includes "END =" followed by a statement number which is the statement to which control is transferred, if an end-of-file is reached. For example,

```
READ(5,101,END=205) A,B,...
```

reads information from the data file, and if an end-of-file is reached (i.e., if there is no more data in the input file), then statement number 205 is executed and the program continues from there. (Essentially a GO TO 205 is performed when EOF is true, cf. Chapter 7). This feature would be particularly useful if someone does not know the amount of information in the input file, and the information is being stored in an array (cf. Chapter 9).

Both the READ and WRITE statements may also include other control information options within the parentheses. See a manual for the version of FORTRAN being used for further information.

3.10 OPEN, CLOSE, AND INQUIRE STATEMENTS

A FORTRAN program automatically "opens" the "standard" input and output "devices" (normally corresponding to device numbers 5 and 6 in the READ/WRITE statements) and prepares them to be used by the program. This is done without any special statements or work by the programmer.

In addition to the "standard" devices, many FORTRAN implementations allow a user to associate arbitrary "device" or "unit" numbers with specific data files, e.g., stored on disk. Sometimes this can be done at execution time, by just listing the device number and the corresponding file name, but usually this must be done from inside the program.

In FORTRAN-77, one can specify input and output files and associate them with user-chosen "device" or "unit" numbers by means of an OPEN statement. To disassociate a given number from a given file, one uses a CLOSE statement.

An OPEN statement consists of the key word OPEN followed by a set of parentheses containing keywords, each followed by an equal sign and a specification according to what the local system demands. More commonly, one need only put in the OPEN statement the most important features, for example, the device number which one wishes to use, the filename which will be associated with that device number, and what type of file it is.

The more common keywords are UNIT (device number), FILE (file name), ACCESS ('SEQUENTIAL' or 'DIRECT'), BLANK ('NULL' or 'ZERO'), STATUS ('OLD' or 'NEW').

A typical invocation of OPEN is as follows:

```
OPEN (UNIT=6,FILE='PROG3.INP',ACCESS=
                'SEQUENTIAL',BLANK='ZERO')
```

This would open file "PROG3.INP" as a sequential file, associate it with number 6 (for use in READ and WRITE statements), and assume that all blanks are to be interpreted as zeroes (cf. Section 4.3).

To disassociate device number 6 from file "PROG3.INP," one could use the command CLOSE(6).

To inquire about the status of a specific device (previously OPENed), one may use the INQUIRE statement, with appropriate (variable) arguments which would store the desired (but presently unknown) information. For example,

```
INQUIRE(FILE='PROG3.INP',OPENED=LOGVAR,NUMBER=N)
```

would return a logical value in variable LOGVAR and an integer value in variable N both of which could be used subsequently in the program.

An OPEN statement needs to be used any time a device number needs to be associated with a file before it is used in a WRITE or READ statement.

The OPEN, CLOSE, and INQUIRE statements may include other control information options within the parentheses. See a manual for the version of FORTRAN being used for further information.

CHAPTER 4

MORE ON FORMATS AND INPUT/OUTPUT

4.1 ADDITIONAL FORMAT FIELD DESCRIPTORS

The following are the other standard field descriptors.

An   Alphanumeric – used for conversion of character data for either output or input:
         n   –   the number of characters associated with the variable, i.e., the field width.

In FORTRAN-77, characters are normally stored in variables declared in CHARACTER type declarations, but in FORTRAN-IV, standard practice is to store characters in INTEGER variables. Further information regarding CHARACTER variables is given in Chapter 11.

Dw.d   Double-Precision – used for real numbers declared as DOUBLE PRECISION:
The same rules hold as for the E field descriptor, except that a D is (usually) printed in the output instead of an E.

Tn   Tabulation:
–on OUTPUT, it is used to tabulate to output space n, which corresponds (because of the carriage control) to

visible column $n-1$. For example, if T30 were to occur in a FORMAT statement immediately before I5, the I5 field would consist of columns 29 through 33.

–on INPUT, the input space and the visible space are the same, so that T30 before I5 would mean that the I5 field would consist of columns 30 through 34. On INPUT, the T descriptor can be used to re-read part or all of the INPUT line.

TLn, TRn (Relative) Tabulation (Left or Right):
–Whereas the Ti field descriptor specifies absolute tabulation to a specific column, the TL (tabulate left) and TR (tabulate right) specify relative tabulation, that is, moving n spaces right or left from the end of the previous field. Thus, TR works exactly the same as the X descriptor. On OUTPUT, TL will *not* cause any overprinting, but on INPUT, it can be used to re-read part or all of the INPUT line.

G General:
used in lieu of E or F. In some implementations, it may also be used in lieu of I, D, and A as well.

Ln Logical:
–on OUTPUT, a T or an F is printed right justified in a field of n blanks.
–on INPUT, n characters are read, and only the first non-blank character is examined. If it is not a T or F (upper or lower case), an error occurs. The T or F may be preceded by a period.

S, SS,SP (Plus) Sign:
–on OUTPUT, SP signals that the numeric descriptors which follow it should print a plus sign before positive numbers. SS signals that the numeric descriptors which

31

follow it should print a blank in lieu of a plus sign. Each descriptor can negate the effect of the other descriptor if more than one descriptor is used successively in one FORMAT statement. The effect of the descriptor lasts only until the end of the FORMAT statement in which it occurs. S returns to the default style of the FORTRAN version being used. (On most systems, S acts like SS.)

nP   scaling factor for F, E, G, or D input or output:
It immediately precedes the key letter of the numeric input descriptor that it scales.
—on INPUT, the number read is multiplied by $10^{**(-n)}$ before storage, unless it contains an explicit exponent.
—on OUTPUT the stored number does not change, but its printed value may not correspond to the internal value. With F editing, the output is the internal value multiplied by 10^{**n}. With D or E editing, the output value is the same as the internal value, but the representation has been shifted so that the exponent is reduced by n, and the mantissa is multiplied by 10^{**n}. With G editing, the effect is based on whether E or F editing is ultimately chosen, in which cases the normal P effect takes place.

The field descriptors mentioned here and above in Section 3.4 are the standard ones used. One should check the manual of the FORTRAN version being used for other possible field descriptors.

4.2 MULTIPLE REPETITIONS

One can use parentheses to induce repetitions of field descriptors within FORMAT statements, even if the field descriptors themselves have repetition factors. For example,

```
FORMAT(3X,3(I10,2F10.5))
```

is equivalent to

```
FORMAT(3X,I10,2F10.5,I10,2F10.5,I10,2F10.5)
```

which itself is equivalent to a FORMAT statement with double the number of F10.5 descriptors in it!

4.3   INPUT FORMAT

Certain care must be taken when working with FORMAT statements associated with READ statements. The following rules should be remembered:

1. There is no carriage control in input;

2. In FORTRAN IV, all blanks are interpreted as zeroes;

3. Any decimal point present in the input supersedes what is suggested by any E, F, D, or G descriptor, otherwise, if no decimal point exists among the input digits, one is "forced" by determining how many digits are to be considered to the right of the (non-existent) decimal point according to the field descriptor;

4. There is no distinction between E, F and G descriptors for input.

In FORTRAN-77, whether (2) holds is system dependent. On some systems, blanks are normally treated as zeroes, but on others, they are ignored. To avoid the uncertainty this may cause, and to allow the programmer to determine how blanks should be interpreted for a particular program, FORTRAN-77 has included two more field descriptors for INPUT use.

BZ, BN   Blanks are Zero (Null):
         –on INPUT, BZ signals that the numeric descriptors which follow it should treat blanks as zeroes. BN signals that the numeric descriptors which follow it should ignore blanks and concatenate all digits together to form the input numeric value. Each descriptor can negate the effect of the other descriptor if more than one descriptor is used successively in one FOR-MAT statement. The effect of the descriptor lasts only until the end of the FORMAT statement in which it occurs.

Note: If a numeric field which follows a BN descriptor contains all blanks, the numeric value is assumed to be zero.

4.4   INPUT FORMAT EXAMPLE

```
        READ(5,101) A,I
 101    FORMAT(BZ,F10.5,I5)
```

Suppose the input line consisted of the following:

```
column number ->
 1  2  3  4  5  6  7  8  9 10 11 12 13 14 15 16
             1  2                       3
```

The variable A would receive the value of 1.2 and I the value of 300.

Explanation:
    Descriptor BZ causes the rest of the FORMAT to treat blanks as zeroes. Field descriptor F10.5 allocates columns 1 through 10

for variable A and says that the last 5 columns will be considered
to the right of the decimal point (unless a decimal point present
forces a different placement). Thus, numbers in columns 6 through
10 are to the right of the decimal point. Therefore, the decimal
point goes between 1 and 2. The next field descriptor I5 allocates
the next five columns, columns 11 through 15 for the next
variable, I. Since columns 14 and 15 are blank, the blanks are
interpreted as zeroes, and I receives the value of 300.

Suppose the following input line was used instead:

```
column number ->
  1   2   3   4   5   6   7   8   9  10  11  12  13  14  15  16
                              1   .   2   3       3       2   3
```

Then A would receive the value of 1.2 and I the value 30302.

Explanation:
    As before, columns 1 through 10 are reserved for variable A.
Since there is now a decimal point included in the input, the 5 in
the field descriptor is ignored. As before, the next five columns are
reserved for the value of I and blanks are interpreted as zeroes.
Thus we get 30302.

The 3 in column 16 is ignored.

4.5   FORMATS: UNDERUSE AND THE COLON FIELD SEPARATOR

Our assumption thus far has been that the number of items
listed in the READ or WRITE statement matches the number of
field descriptors found in the corresponding FORMAT statement.
In general, this does not have to be the case. It is permitted to have
fewer or more field descriptors in a FORMAT statement than

35

variables in the corresponding input or output statement. However, in either case special rules apply.

If there are fewer variables than format field descriptors, the READ or WRITE uses as many as are needed to print out all the variables, and then ignores the rest of the descriptors in the FORMAT statement. Thus, the following is legal FORTRAN code:

```
      WRITE(6,101)  I,J,K
      WRITE(6,101)  L,M,N1,N2,N3
101   FORMAT(1X,10I5)
```

Note that there are more than enough numeric field descriptors (10 integer fields) in FORMAT 101 for either WRITE statement.

If the FORMAT statement has a literal character string in it immediately before the first field descriptor which is not being used, the literal character string will still be printed out! In other words,

```
      I = 2
      WRITE(6,101)  I
101   FORMAT(1X,'I=',I2,' and J=',I2)
```

will print out:

```
      I=2 and J=
```

In general, FORTRAN will continue to try to use field descriptors until nothing is left in the READ/WRITE statement. However, if it is desirable to omit printing the second literal character string, one can precede the string with a colon, :, instead of a comma. In other words,

```
        I = 2
        WRITE(6,101) I
  101   FORMAT(1X,'I=',I2:' and J=',I2)
```

will print out:

```
  I=2
```

4.6 FORMATS: OVERUSE

If there are more variables than FORMAT field descriptors, then the FORMAT statement is re-used until all the variables are either READ into or WRITTEN out. As usual, each re-use of the associated FORMAT statement starts a new input/output line.

Let us look at the following example.

```
        WRITE(6,102) A1,A2,A3,A4,B1,B2,B3,B4
  102   FORMAT(1X,2F20.5)
```

Here, FORMAT 102 only provides for two numeric fields. However, the WRITE statement contains eight variables. Therefore, FORMAT 102 gets re-used 4 times, each time starting a new line (because of the blank carriage control character induced by the initial 1X). However, if FORMAT 102 were changed to allow three numbers per line, the output would consist of three lines, with three variables per line for the first two lines, and two variables on the last line. The order of the variables would be the same, i.e., A1, then A2, then A3, then A4, then B1, then B2, then B3, and finally B4.

There is one minor variation of the re-use rule when the FORMAT statement itself contains parentheses (used for multiple repetitions, e.g., 3(2I5,3F10.5)). In these cases, the entire

FORMAT statement is *not* re-used. Only the last parenthesized multiple repetition to the end of the format is re-used. For example, if the following format has to be re-used:

```
103   FORMAT(1X, I5, (1X,2F10.5))
```

then the first line would have three numbers on it (corresponding to I5, F10.5, and F10.5) and the remaining (repetition) lines would only have two numbers on them (corresponding to what is in the (last and only) group repetition) even though it has no preceding repetition factor).

4.7 "FORMAT-FREE" INPUT AND OUTPUT (FORTRAN-77)

FORTRAN-77 has standardized the extensions which have been used for some years by some versions of FORTRAN-IV and allows the use of an asterisk (*) instead of a FORMAT statement number in a READ or WRITE statement. This causes the compiler to match the appropriate field descriptor (of appropriate size) to the variable (or constant) in the variable list of the READ/WRITE statement.

For example,

```
WRITE(6,*)  I,A,B,J
```

or

```
READ(5,*)  A,B,J
```

or

```
WRITE(6,*)  ' I =',I
```

4.8 OTHER INPUT AND OUTPUT COMMANDS

Other input/output commands exist in FORTRAN-77 and in local dialects of FORTRAN-IV. Often they omit the use of a device number and/or the FORMAT number, since frequently they specify one particular device.

For example,

```
PRINT n, <variable list> - directly print
                           on printer
TYPE n,  <variable list> - directly type
                           on terminal
PUNCH n, <variable list> - punch onto
                           IBM cards
```

where *n* is the FORMAT statement number.

In addition, file positioning statements are also available, which are especially useful when using magnetic tapes, but can be applied to any sequential access external file. These statements are:

```
BACKSPACE n  - position file before
               previous record

ENDFILE n    - write end of file record

REWIND   n   - position file at beginning
```

where *n* is the unit number of the file.

CHAPTER 5

COUNTED LOOPS (DO-LOOPS)

5.1 THE CONTINUE STATEMENT

The CONTINUE statement does absolutely nothing. It functions as a convenient statement on which to tack a statement number.

```
      7+
10004 CONTINUE
```

5.2 COUNTED LOOPS

The counted loop in FORTRAN is normally referred to by its key word, DO. Its general form is as follows:

```
7+
DO n IVAR = begval,endval,step
```

FORTRAN-77 also allows:

```
DO n , IVAR = begval,endval,step
```

The number *n* which follows the DO is the statement number

of the last statement to be executed in the loop, and must be an integer constant. The last statement must be executable, and thus, cannot be a FORMAT or an END (among others).

Contemporary programming style suggests that all DO loops should end with a CONTINUE statement, and that all statements interior to the loop be indented to make the code more readable. However, the definition of FORTRAN permits the final statement in a DO loop to be any executable statement.

IVAR can be any (integer) variable and is the loop counter. This variable can be used within the loop, but no attempt should be made to try to change its value. Some compilers will give an error if this variable is used on the left of an assignment statement within the loop. Officially, the loop variable will be undefined when the loop is completed.

FORTRAN-77 permits the optional presence of a comma between the statement number n and the loop counter variable IVAR. Using this comman can avoid errors of the type mentioned below in section 5.5.

Begval, endval, step can be (integer) constants or variables which correspond to the beginning value of the loop variable, the ending value, and the step size.

If the step constant (or variable) is omitted (with its preceding comma), the step size is assumed to be 1.

Note: In FORTRAN-IV, these three values had to be POSI-TIVE INTEGERS, and could *not* be expressions. However, in FORTRAN-77, the variable and values may be REAL or even DOUBLE PRECISION, and the values may be negative or zero. The values may also be determined by expressions (which are evaluated before the loop starts execution and converted [by

41

truncation] to integer quantities if the variable is INTEGER). Note that a negative step allows a "counting down."

5.3 LOOP OPERATION

The FORTRAN DO-loop operates as follows: the counter variable is assigned the beginning value, and then is modified according to the step size after each execution of the loop. The looping action stops when the counter variable has a value outside the ending range specified by the ending value.

In FORTRAN-IV, the test is performed at the end of the loop. As a result, even if the beginning value and ending value are inconsistent (e.g., DO 10 I=5,1,2), the loop is done at least once.

In FORTRAN-77, the test is performed at the beginning of the loop. Thus, depending on whether there is a positive step size or not, the loop may or may not be done. For example, DO 10 I=5,1,2 would not be done at all, but DO 10 I=5, 1,–2 would be done 3 times (with I having the values of 5, 3, and 1).

5.4 EXAMPLE

```
      A = 0.0
      DO 10 I=1,20
         A=A+1.0
10    CONTINUE
```

This piece of code would perform the assignment statement within the loop 20 times, adding 1.0 to the previous value of A each time. Thus, at the end of this piece of code, the variable A would have the value of 20.0.

Note: Many FORTRAN compilers provide options which allow users to determine whether they wish DO loops in their programs to run according to FORTRAN-IV or FORTRAN-77 rules, thereby making old programs which run on new compilers give the same results. Only a relatively few programs would be affected by the change of rules.

5.5 WARNING

The FORTRAN convention that blanks are ignored and that undeclared variables have a default type can lead to unexpected and undesirable results. On July 22, 1963, the U.S. Mariner I rocket was launched at Cape Canaveral on the first mission to Venus. It started veering toward earth and was destroyed at a cost of $18.5 million. The reason was due to a period being mistakenly typed in place of a comma in a DO statement.

Suppose one omits the step size and changes the comma to a period in a DO loop statement. In other words, instead of writing

```
DO 10 I = 1, 10
```

suppose one writes

```
DO 10 I = 1. 10
```

The first statement is a valid DO loop header. But to analyze the second statement, we first recall that blanks are ignored, that variables do not have to be declared before use, and that the data type of an undeclared variable is determined (by default) according to the first letter. If we re-write the second statement after omitting blanks, we get

```
DO10I=1.10
```

which now can be seen to be an assignment statement (rather than a DO loop header), giving the (default type) REAL variable DO10I the value of 1.10. Thus, instead of the interior statements of what was thought to be a loop being performed 10 times, they would be done only once, and could lead to answers drastically different than what was expected.

5.6 NESTED DO LOOPS

In some other contemporary languages, it is impossible to incorrectly nest counted loops because of language features which automatically close off the nearest (unclosed) loop. However, in FORTRAN, one must be careful that, when nesting counted loops, one loop is contained entirely within another.

For example, the following is incorrect FORTRAN, and would give a compiler error.

```
          DO 10 I=1,10
          DO 20 J=1,20
          . . .
10        CONTINUE
20        CONTINUE
```

The beginnings and endings of different loops cannot overlap each other.

On the other hand, the following is perfectly good FOR-TRAN.

```
          DO 110 I=1,10
              DO 120 J=1,20
              . . .
120           CONTINUE
110       CONTINUE
```

Note that in this second case, the interior loop (DO 120 ...) begins and ends totally within the range of the first loop.

Note also the effect of this construction. For each pass of the outer loop (the "110 I" loop), the inner loop is completely executed (all 20 times). Therefore, the statements interior to the inner loop are (in this case) executed a total of 200 (10*20) times.

5.7 EXAMPLE: COMPLETE FORTRAN PROGRAM

```
      PROGRAM TEST
C
C     PROGRAM TO CREATE A CONVERSION
C     CHART CONVERTING MILES TO KILOMETERS
C     FROM 5 MILES TO 60 MILES
C
C     VARIABLE DECLARATIONS
C
      INTEGER NUM
      REAL MILES,KILOS,EIGHT5
C
C     INITIALIZATION AND HEADER
C
      EIGHT5=8.0/5.0
      WRITE(6,100)
100   FORMAT(7X,'Miles',3X,'Kilometers')
C
C     LOOP TO CONVERT MILES TO KILOMETERS
C
      DO 20 NUM=5,60,5
         MILES=NUM
         KILOS=MILES*EIGHT5
         WRITE(6,101) MILES,KILOS
101      FORMAT(1X,2F10.1)
20    CONTINUE
      STOP
      END
```

CHAPTER 6

LIBRARY FUNCTIONS

6.1 OVERVIEW

Most of the standard mathematical functions exist as library functions in FORTRAN. In addition, there exist functions to covert from one data type to another.

There usually exists more than one FORTRAN function to do the same thing, but which function a programmer uses depends on the data type of the argument(s) and which return type is desired. For example, ABS and IABS are both absolute value functions, taking one argument, but according to default typing, ABS is real and is used for a real argument (returning a real result), and IABS is integer, and is used for an integer argument (returning an integer result).

FORTRAN-77 also includes 'generic' functions which eliminate the necessity of having to choose the proper function name to match the argument's or output value's type. In most cases, the output type of these 'generic' functions adjusts to match the input type. The older, specific names, proper to each data type, may continue to be used, and in many cases, insure greater portability of the resulting program code.

The standard FORTRAN-77 functions are listed below (with their argument type and output type). Some implementations have their own additional library functions and programmers should check the manuals of the version they are using for further information.

In the following list, function names may be preceded by a 77 or an E. The 77 indicates that this function exists in the standard list of FORTRAN-77 library functions, but *not* in the standard list of FORTRAN-IV functions. Thus, it may not be available on older compilers – the user should consult the local manuals when in doubt. In addition, certain older or small scale compilers do not implement COMPLEX numbers or DOUBLE PRECISION numbers; hence, the corresponding functions are not available.

The E indicates that this functions was designated an EXTERNAL function in FORTRAN-IV, and thus could be used as an argument to a FUNCTION or a SUBROUTINE. In FORTRAN-77, all library functions may be thus used, and so are called 'intrinsic.' Cf. also Chapter 10, section 10.8.

6.2 TABLE OF STANDARD LIBRARY FUNCTIONS

In the ARGUMENT TYPE and OUTPUT TYPE columns of the following table, R indicates REAL, I indicates INTEGER, DP indicates DOUBLE PRECISION, C indicates COMPLEX, Char indicates Character, and L indicates LOGICAL.

Note: If a generic name is missing in the last column, then the specific function name still works in FORTRAN-77, but that function name cannot be used other than in the case listed, i.e., with the data types listed for the argument(s) and output.

	Function Name	Argument Type	Output Type	Fortran-77 Generic Name
General Functions				
	Absolute Value			
	ABS	R	R	ABS
	IABS	I	I	ABS
	DABS	DP	DP	ABS
E	CABS	C	R	ABS

(**Note:** in this last case, the result is the mathematical magnitude of a complex number, i.e., the straight line distance of the point from the origin.)

	Function Name	Argument Type	Output Type	Fortran-77 Generic Name
	Greatest Integer (Truncation)			
	AINT	R	R	AINT
77	DINT	DP	DP	AINT
	IDINT	DP	I	INT
	INT	R	I	INT
	Nearest Whole Number (Rounding)			
77	ANINT	R	R	ANINT
77	DNINT	DP	DP	ANINT
77	NINT	R	I	NINT
77	IDNINT	DP	I	NINT
	Remainder after Division			
	AMOD	R (2 arg.)	R	MOD
	MOD	I (2 arg.)	I	MOD
E	DMOD	DP (2 arg.)	DP	MOD
	Transfer of Sign from First Argument to the Second			
	ISIGN	I (2 arg.)	I	SIGN
	SIGN	R (2 arg.)	R	SIGN
	DSIGN	DP (2 arg.)	DP	SIGN

Function Name	Argument Type	Output Type	Fortran-77 Generic Name
Maximum (multiple arguments possible)			
AMAX0	I	R	–
AMAX1	R	R	MAX
MAX0	I	I	MAX
MAX1	R	I	–
DMAX1	DP	DP	MAX

Minimum (same as MAX function except substitute 'MIN' for 'MAX')

Type Conversion Functions (cf. Chapter 12, section 12.3 for the discussion of Complex Functions.)

FLOAT	I	R	REAL
IFIX	R	I	INT
SNGL	DP	R	REAL
DBLE	R,I	DP	DBLE
(Real part of a complex number)			
REAL	C	R	REAL
(Integer equivalent of the real part of a complex number)			
INT	C	I	INT
(Double precision equivalent of the real part of a complex number)			
DBLE	C	DP	DBLE

49

	Function Name	Argument Type	Output Type	Fortran-77 Generic Name
	(Imaginary part of a complex number)			
	AIMAG	C	R	–
	CMPLX	R (2 arg.)	C	CMPLX
	CMPLX	I, DP (2 arg.)	C	CMPLX

(**Note**: in this case, the I or DP values are first converted to R.)

	Function Name	Argument Type	Output Type	Fortran-77 Generic Name
	CMPLX	R,I,DP (1 arg.)	C	CMPLX

(**Note**: in this case, the second argument is assumed to be 0.)

	Function Name	Argument Type	Output Type	Fortran-77 Generic Name
	CONJG	C	C	–

Mathematical Functions

	Function Name	Argument Type	Output Type	Fortran-77 Generic Name
	Square Root			
E	SQRT	R	R	SQRT
E	DSQRT	DP	DP	SQRT
E	CSQRT	C	C	SQRT
	Exponential (e=2.718281828 ... raised to a power)			
E	EXP	R	R	EXP
E	DEXP	DP	DP	EXP
E	CEXP	C	C	EXP
	Natural Logarithm (Base e)			
E	ALOG	R	R	LOG
E	DLOG	DP	DP	LOG
E	CLOG	C	C	LOG

	Function Name	Argument Type	Output Type	Fortran-77 Generic Name
	Logarithm Base 10			
E	ALOG10	R	R	LOG10
E	DLOG10	DP	DP	LOG10
	Positive Difference (i.e., DIM(x,y) returns MAX($x-y$,0)			
	IDIM	I (2 arg.)	I	DIM
	DIM	R (2 arg.)	R	DIM
77	DDIM	DP (2 arg.)	DP	DIM
	Double Precision Product of Two Real Arguments			
77	DPROD	R (2 arg.)	D	–
Trigonometric Functions–Argument/Answer in radian measure				
E	SIN	R	R	SIN
E	DSIN	DP	DP	SIN
E	CSIN	C	C	SIN
E	COS	R	R	COS
E	DCOS	DP	DP	COS
E	CCOS	C	C	COS
77	TAN	R	R	TAN
77	DTAN	DP	DP	TAN
	Inverse Sine (Arcsine)			
77	ASIN	R	R	ASIN
77	DASIN	DP	DP	ASIN
	Inverse Cosine			
77	ACOS	R	R	ACOS
77	DACOS	DP	DP	ACOS

	Function Name	Argument Type	Output Type	Fortran-77 Generic Name
	Inverse Tangent			
E	ATAN	R	R	ATAN
E	DATAN	DP	DP	ATAN
	Inverse Tangent of QUOTIENT of 2 arguments			
E	ATAN2	R	R	ATAN2
E	DATAN2	DP	DP	ATAN2
	Hyperbolic Sine			
77	SINH	R	R	SINH
77	DSINH	DP	DP	SINH
	Hyperbolic Cosine			
77	COSH	R	R	COSH
77	DCOSH	DP	DP	COSH
	Hyperbolic Tangent			
E	TANH	R	R	TANH
77	DTANH	DP	DP	TANH

Character Functions (See Chapter 11, section 11.6 for more discussion.)

77	LEN	Char	I	–
77	INDEX	Char (2 arg.)	I	–
77	ICHAR	Char	I	–
77	CHAR	I	Char	–
77	LGE	Char (2 arg.)	L	–
77	LGT	Char (2 arg.)	L	–
77	LLE	Char (2 arg.)	L	–
77	LLT	Char (2 arg.)	L	–

6.3 EXAMPLES

As mentioned above, the library FUNCTIONS are merely used in an arithmetic expression as they might be used in algebra. For example,

```
AROOT = (-B + SQRT(B*B-4*A*C))/(2*A)
X = 2*SIN(THETA)*COS(THETA)
```

CHAPTER 7

GO TO'S

7.1 UNCONDITIONAL GO TO'S

There are two major types of GO TO's in FORTRAN, unconditional GO TO's and computed GO TO's. A third type of GO TO (infrequently used) is mentioned in section 14.3.

The form of the unconditional GO TO is as follows:

```
7+
GO TO n
```

where *n* is an integer number which is used as the statement label of an executable statement (including a CONTINUE) (thus, FORMAT statements and END statements are excluded). The statement transferred to must be in the same program segment (i.e., it cannot be in a different subprogram).

The program flow is transferred unconditionally to statement number *n* and continues from there. This is *not* the same as a SUBROUTINE call which comes back to the line after the point from which it is called. Once control is transferred to another statement by means of a GO TO, the only way control can get back to the point of the program after the GO TO in question is by means of another GO TO!

For example,

```
   PROGRAM SAM7
   WRITE(6,*) 'Point 1'
   GO TO 1
2  WRITE(6,*) 'Point 2'
   STOP
1  WRITE(6,*) 'Point 3'
   GO TO 2
   END
```

will cause the output

```
   Point 1
   Point 3
   Point 2
```

because of the leap-frog program flow.

7.2 COMPUTED GO TO'S

The form of the computed GO TO is as follows:

```
7+
GO TO (n1,n2,...,nk),INTVAR
```

where $n1$, $n2$, ..., nk are integer numbers (less than 99,999) used as statement labels, and INTVAR is any integer variable which evaluates to some integer from 1 to k inclusive.

If INTVAR evaluates to 1, then control is transferred to statement $n1$. Similarly, if INTVAR evaluates to 2, control is transferred to statement $n2$. It is as if the computed GO TO reduces to the unconditional GO TO *nk* if INTVAR evaluates to *k*. Note that $n1, \ldots, nk$ do not have to be in any numeric order or any order as far as their occurrence in the program segment is concerned (see example below).

In FORTRAN-77, the comma between the closing parenthesis and the variable can be omitted, and the variable may be replaced by an integer expression.

Note: Possible problems can arise if INTVAR < 1 or INTVAR > *k*. In general, what happens to the computed GO TO in these cases is undetermined, although local implementations may have specific rules. Some compilers may give run-time errors if an out-of-range variable is detected. Some implementations determine that if INTVAR <= 1, control goes to statement *n1*, and if INTVAR >= *k*, control goes to statement *nk*. Finally, some implementations determine that if INTVAR is not in the acceptable range, a GO TO is not executed, and control continues with the statement following the GO TO.

7.3 PROBLEMS WITH GO TO'S

Since control transfers elsewhere in a program because of a GO TO, the statement following a GO TO must be labeled (except if it is an END), and somewhere in the program there must be a GO TO leading back to that statement, or else it will never be executed! Some compilers give errors if statements following GO TO's are not labeled, others do not.

As the example above shows, GO TO's can also lead to messy and unreadable code. Code containing many GO TO's is often called "spaghetti code," since frequently its flow is about as apparent as a bowl of spaghetti. With FORTRAN-77 structures, there is less need to use GO TO's, although, if used in a disciplined, structured, and documented manner, no difficulty should be encountered.

In particular, GO TO's should never be used to jump into or out of any loops, particularly DO loops. In general, programs should be written so that loops are entered only from their "top," and exited only from their "bottom." Premature exit from loops may lead to disaster. Thus GO TO's should normally be used only to imitate structures available in other languages which have not yet been implemented in FORTRAN.

7.4 EXAMPLE: TRANSLATING A PASCAL "CASE" STATEMENT

As an example of a disciplined (and somewhat necessary) use of both forms of GO TO's, look at the following translation of a Pascal (or C) CASE statement. The CASE statement provides a single choice between multiple options based on a key variable. In the example below, if the variable I has the value of 2 before beginning the CASE structure, only the statements comprising <block2> would be done – all other blocks would be skipped.

```
      PASCAL
case i of
   1:<block1>;
   2:<block2>;
   3:<block3>;
   4:<block4>
end;


      FORTRAN EQUIVALENT
C     CASE
      GO TO (101,102,105,103),I
101   <block1>
```

57

```
        GO TO 104
102     <block2>
        GO TO 104
105     <block3>
        GO TO 104
103     <block4>
C       END CASE
104     CONTINUE
```

Comment: If I had the value of 3 in the FORTRAN code, the third label listed in the computed GO TO would be chosen, i.e., 105, and a 'GO TO 105' would (in effect) be performed. After all the statements comprising <block3> were done, the GO TO 104 would skip over the statements comprising <block4> and the program would continue with statement 104 and those which follow it.

CHAPTER 8

LOGICAL EXPRESSIONS AND IF STATEMENTS

8.1   LOGICAL RELATIONAL OPERATORS

FORTRAN uses the term LOGICAL to designate variables, constants and expressions whose values are either true or false. Mathematicians and some other computer languages refer to these as "boolean" values. Since special symbols were non-existent on card punch machines, in early versions of FORTRAN, logical operators had to be represented by letters instead of symbols. However, to distinguish between letter combinations used as logical operators and letter combinations used as "normal" variables, FORTRAN required that logical operations and constants be surrounded by periods.

Thus the relational operators (and their mathematical symbolic and verbal equivalents) are:

.EQ.	=	is equal to
.LT.	<	is less than
.LE.	<=	is less than or equal to
.GT.	>	is greater than
.GE.	>=	is greater than or equal to
.NE.	<>	is not equal to

Note: the symbolic equivalents are not standard options in most FORTRAN implementations. They are listed for comparisons with other computer languages.

The logical constants are:

.TRUE.   .FALSE.

The other operators are:

.AND.   .OR.   .NOT.
.EQV.   (for logical equivalence)
.NEQV.   (for not equivalent)

Note: The standard rules of logic hold for evaluating FORTRAN LOGICAL expressions.

- If A and B are logical expressions, A .AND. B is .TRUE. only if both A and B are .TRUE.

- A .OR. B is .TRUE. only if either A or B or both are .TRUE.

- A .EQV. B is .TRUE. only if both A and B are .TRUE. or both A and B are .FALSE.

- A .NEQV. B is .TRUE. only if one is .TRUE. and the other is .FALSE.

As is common for the rules of logic, .NOT. is evaluated before the others, .AND. takes precedence over .OR., and .EQV. and .NEQV. are performed last.

In addition, FORTRAN logical expressions must be surrounded by parentheses when used in other structures.

8.2   DECISION STATEMENTS
(IF STATEMENTS)

The only class of decision statement in FORTRAN is the IF statement. There are several types of IF statements in FORTRAN-77, most of which were inherited from FORTRAN-IV.

8.3   ARITHMETIC IF

This is the oldest form of decision statement in FORTRAN and uses an ARITHMETIC expression on which to base a decision.

Its form is as follows:

```
7+
IF ( <arithmetic expression> ) n1, n2, n3
```

The operation of this IF is as follows: if the arithmetic expression evaluates to a negative number, control is transferred to statement labeled $n1$. If the arithmetic expression evaluates to zero, control is transferred to statement labeled $n2$. If the arithmetic expression evaluates to a positive number, control is transferred to statement labeled $n3$.

Since this form of the IF is equivalent to 3 GO TO's, the same rule holds as for GO TO's, namely, that the statement following an arithmetic IF must have a statement label.

As a simple example,

```
      IF(A)10,15,15
10    ABSA=-A
      GO TO 20
```

```
15     ABSA=A
20     CONTINUE
```

is one way to implement an absolute value function. If A had the value of − 2.5, control would transfer to statement 10, ABSA would receive the value of − (− 2.5), i.e., 2.5, and then control would transfer to statement 20.

8.4   ONE STATEMENT LOGICAL IF

If one needs to do only one thing (e.g., a subroutine call, an assignment statement), based on the evaluation of a logical expression, one can use the one statement version of the logical IF.

Its form is as follows:

```
7+
IF ( <logical condition> ) statement
```

In this case, if the logical condition evaluates to .TRUE. the statement is executed. If the condition evaluates to .FALSE. the statement is ignored and control continues with the next statement following.

For example, another way to implement an absolute value function is as follows:

```
IF (ABSA) .LT. 0.0) ABSA = −ABSA
```

Note: In this example, the test condition is based on the evaluation of the LOGICAL relational expression ABSA .LT. 0.0. If it is .TRUE. in a given instance, then the remainder of the statement is performed.

62

8.5 BLOCK IF (FORTRAN-77)

FORTRAN-77 has added the version of the IF statement commonly called the BLOCK IF which has become common in other contemporary structured languages or special earlier versions of FORTRAN.

Its form is:

```
7+
IF (A .LE. B) THEN
    <block1>
ELSE
    <block2>
ENDIF
```

As many statements as needed can be included in <block1> or <block2>. If the boolean expression evaluates to .TRUE., then <block1> is done and <block2> is ignored. If the boolean expression evaluates to .FALSE., then <block2> is done and <block1> is ignored. After executing the statements in the chosen block, control transfers to the next statement following the ENDIF.

If the ELSE section is not needed, it can be omitted. The IF statement then can take on this form:

```
7+
IF (A .LE. B) THEN
    <block>
ENDIF
```

If repeated conditions need to be checked, one can expand the ELSE section by adding IF on the same line, and using only one

ENDIF. As many ELSE IF lines as needed can be used. For example,

```
7+
IF (A .LE. B) THEN
    <block1>
ELSE IF (A .GT. C) THEN
    <block2>
ELSE
    <block3>
ENDIF
```

Note: If the second IF were placed on a separate line (and not combined with the first ELSE), then two separate ENDIFs would be necessary.

8.6   TWO VALUE LOGICAL IF

The two value IF was commonly used in FORTRAN IV to implement what a BLOCK IF does in FORTRAN-77 but in a less structured way. Its form is

```
7+
IF (A .LE. B) n1, n2
```

If the condition evaluates to .TRUE. then control is transferred to statement label $n1$. However, if the condition evaluates to .FALSE. then control is transferred to statement label $n2$. As with the arithmetic IF mentioned above, this is equivalent to two GO TO's, and as such, any statement immediately following this IF must have a statement label.

Note that since the BLOCK IF structure provides equivalent program control with better readability, some versions of FORTRAN-77 do not support the two-value IF.

8.7 EXAMPLE: TRANSLATION OF "WHILE" LOOP

An IF and a GO TO can be used in a structured manner to imitate the function of a (conditional) "while" loop found in many other languages.

```
PASCAL

while(a < b) do
    begin
        . . .
    end


FORTRAN EQUIVALENT

10   IF(.NOT.(A .LT. B)) GO TO 20
        . . .
     GO TO 10
20   CONTINUE


     -or-


10   IF(A .LT. B) THEN
        . . .
        GO TO 10
     END IF
```

CHAPTER 9

ARRAYS

9.1 OVERVIEW

As with many other languages, in FORTRAN arrays are a way of storing many pieces of information (i.e., associating a number of variables) under one name. The concept corresponds to the use of subscripted variables in mathematics, e.g., x_1, x_2, ..., x_{10}. Variables are associated together because of one name, but they can be distinguished because of different subscripts.

9.2 DECLARING ONE DIMENSIONAL ARRAYS (DIMENSION STATEMENTS)

In FORTRAN, array variables must always be declared before use. In FORTRAN-IV, the array subscript value had to start at 1, but in FORTRAN-77, any INTEGER is permitted as the starting subscript value.

Arrays may be declared in two different ways. One may declare an array in a regular type statement. Or, one may use a DIMENSION statement, whose sole purpose is to declare arrays and their dimensions. In either case the procedure is the same: the variable name is listed, and the size of the array is indicated by being enclosed in parentheses. For example, if one wishes B to be

66

a REAL array of size 20 (with first subscript equal to 1), then one can just write

```
REAL B(20)
```

or, using a DIMENSION statement and default typing,

```
DIMENSION B(20)
```

or, using a DIMENSION statement and explicit typing,

```
REAL   B
DIMENSION B(20)
```

Notes:

1. Most contemporary authors suggest that the DIMENSION statement should never be used by contemporary programmers, since it lets people rely on default variable typing, which is a common source of errors.

2. An array cannot be dimensioned more than once in the same program segment. Thus, for example, a programmer should never put B(20) both in a REAL statement and in a DIMENSION statement. In the third example above, the array B was listed without its subscript in the type statement and with the subscript in the DIMENSION statement.

In FORTRAN-77, if a programmer wishes to have the low subscript start at a number other than one, the programmer indicates both the low and high subscripts, separated by a colon, within the parentheses after the variable name when declaring the array. For example, if we wanted the array B to be of size 20, but the low subscript to be − 10, we could write

```
REAL B(-10:9)
```

9.3   ACCESSING ARRAY ELEMENTS

One accesses an element of an array by indicating the array name followed by the subscript in parentheses. The subscript may be an integer constant, integer variable, or integer expression. For example,

```
A = B(2) + B(3)*4.0
```

Note: In FORTRAN-77, any INTEGER expression may be used. In older versions of FORTRAN, the expression had to have the form

```
    variable plus (or minus) constant
-or-
    constant times variable
-or-
    constant1 times variable plus (or minus)
    constant2
```

With these restrictions, A(3*I) would be legal, but A(I*3) would be illegal, since the order of the constant and the variable are reversed.

9.4   SAMPLE PROGRAM SEGMENT

The following segment shows the standard code which is used to add up the elements of an array B (with 10 elements) and store the sum in variable SUM.

```
        SUM = 0.0
        DO 10 I=1,10
            SUM = SUM + B(I)
10      CONTINUE
```

9.5 WARNING: MISLEADING ERROR MESSAGES

FORTRAN uses parentheses in at least three different ways – for arrays, in arithmetic expressions, and to enclose function and subroutine parameters. The compiler can confuse these usages when the programmer makes an error by forgetting a required array declaration, or by mistyping a variable name, or in some other way.

Undeclared arrays can lead to confusing error messages from compilers. Suppose B is assumed to be an array and is used in an assignment statement, e.g., A = 2*B(I). Suppose that, by oversight, B was not declared as an **array**. The compiler should detect an error at this point, and many compilers will give the error message: "unknown FUNCTION B encountered." To understand the error message, one should examine the form of an array element, e.g., B(I) – it is an identifier, followed by another identifier in parentheses. Since this form is the same form used in a FUNCTION call, most compilers consider the first identifier to actually be a FUNCTION. The compiler then looks for the (nonexistent) FUNCTION in its lists of library and user-defined FUNCTIONS, and finding none by that name, gives an unknown FUNCTION error message.

Another common error case happens when a programmer forgets the FORTRAN multiplication sign (*) between a variable and an expression surrounded by parentheses. For example, one might type

```
A = 2.0*B(I+J-3)
```

rather than

```
A = 2.0*B*(I+J-3)
```

and, since what was typed looks like a function call or an array, as in the previous case one may get an error message which seems to be unrelated to the actual error.

9.6   HIGHER DIMENSIONAL ARRAYS

To declare a two or higher dimensional array, one lists the identifier with all the high end subscripts (separated by commas) in a variable type statement (or use a DIMENSION statement). If the subscripts will not all start at one, the programmer can follow the same pattern shown above in the one dimension case, namely, indicate both low and high subscripts separated by a colon, for each dimension. For example,

```
REAL NUM(3,3,5), NAMES(5:10,1:30)
```

In this example, NUM is a three-dimensional array with $3 \times 3 \times 5 = 45$ variables declared, and NAMES is a two-dimensional array with $6 \times 30 = 180$ variables declared.

FORTRAN-77 allows a maximum of 7 subscripts, and FORTRAN-IV only allows a maximum of 3 subscripts. However, many local implementations allow more.

Two dimensional arrays are frequently used as tables to store information in rows and columns. The first subscript is usually associated with the row, and the second subscript is associated with the column. Two dimensional arrays are regularly used to store matrices used in mathematical problems.

Three dimensional arrays are often visualized as having rows, columns and levels, but no suitable visualization exists for four or higher dimensional arrays.

9.7 STORAGE OF MULTI-DIMENSIONAL ARRAYS

The way that two and higher dimensional arrays are stored internally in computer memory can be important in certain special situations, for example, input and output.

FORTRAN stores arrays in what is called "column major" order. In other words, using the two-dimensional case as an example, the first column of the table (or matrix) is totally stored (in consecutive memory locations) before the second column is stored, and the second column before the third, etc.

For example, the INTEGER array L(3,4) may be visualized as a table or matrix with 3 rows and 4 columns, as follows:

L(1,1)	L(1,2)	L(1,3)	L(1,4)
L(2,1)	L(2,2)	L(2,3)	L(2,4)
L(3,1)	L(3,2)	L(3,3)	L(3,4)

The FORTRAN order of storage is L(1,1) followed by L(2,1) (which is the second element in the first column), followed by L(3,1) (which is the third and last element in the first column), followed by L(1,2) (which is the first element in the next column), followed by L(2,2), L(3,2), L(1,3), L(2,3), L(3,3), L(1,4), L(2,4), and finally L(3,4).

FORTRAN "column major" storage differs from the usual intuitive approach most people take in identifying the "next" element in a two-dimensional array (or matrix). The "human" order is "row major," i.e., the first row is stored (consecutively) before the next row. In the previous example, the (human or row-major) order of the storage of elements of L would be L(1,1), L(1,2), L(1,3), L(1,4), L(2,1) L(2,2), L(2,3), L(2,4), L(3,1) L(3,2), L(3,3) and finally L(3,4). This is also the internal order used in

71

several other computer languages. This difference between the two orders can cause problems if one writes a FORTRAN SUBROUTINE which is to be used with a main program written in a different language and one wishes to pass arrays back and forth.

The standard rule of thumb used to decipher the order in which an array of any dimension is stored by FORTRAN is this: the first subscript varies the fastest. That is, in determining the changing of subscripts, the order is opposite from the order used on a digital clock or a mileage odometer in a car. For example, suppose A was declared as follows:

```
REAL A(3,4,2)
```

then, in memory, the next location after the one containing A(1,3,1) would contain A(2,3,1), then A(3,3,1), then A(1,4,1). After A(3,4,1) would come A(1,1,2), and so on.

9.8 ONE-DIMENSIONAL ARRAYS AND INPUT AND OUTPUT

The standard rule for FORTRAN input/output is that each invocation of a READ/WRITE starts a new line/card according to the format specified in the related FORMAT statement. Therefore, the following program would read five lines, one number per line:

```
      DO 10 I=1,5,1
         READ(5,101) A(I)
101      FORMAT(F10.5)
10    CONTINUE
```

However, if one wanted to read more than one bit of information on one line, that fact needs to be indicated in the READ statement (and associated FORMAT statement).

The basic presupposition is that each READ statement (or each re-use in a loop of a READ statement) starts a new input line.

Therefore, if one wanted to read five numbers on one line, one would have to write the following:

```
      READ(5,101)  A(1),A(2),A(3),A(4),A(5)
101   FORMAT(5F10.5)
```

One can simplify the notation by using an "IMPLIED DO-LOOP" construction as follows:

```
      READ(5,101)  (A(I),I=1,5)
101   FORMAT(5F10.5)
```

Note that the "DO LOOP" variable and its limits (with a step if desired) must be associated with a variable by means of parentheses. Essentially, the implied DO-loop expression is "expanded" to full form, and then the READ is executed.

If the array A is declared to be of dimension 5, one can omit the subscript and implied DO loop entirely. For example, one can write

```
      READ(5,101)  A
101   FORMAT(5F10.5)
```

In this last case, (assuming that A was properly declared as an array) FORTRAN would know that A is an array rather than a scalar variable, and automatically "expand" A to its full dimension before executing the READ. Thus the three different examples given above would be equivalent!

Note: This same discussion also holds for output using WRITE statements.

9.9 MULTI-DIMENSIONAL ARRAYS AND INPUT AND OUTPUT

Multi-dimensional arrays can cause programmers problems when these arrays are used in automatic input and output, unless the programmer remembers that the FORTRAN storage order differs from the programmer's "human" order, as described in Section 9.5.

Suppose A is dimensioned as REAL A(3,4). Then A has three "rows" and four "columns" if we think in terms of a table or matrix. Since FORTRAN stores the array in column order, this is the order which is used in "automatic" input or output (i.e. the third example above without any subscripts). Therefore, if one omits the subscript, for example:

```
WRITE(6,101) A
```

then the order in which the elements of the two dimensional array would appear would be FORTRAN column order (rather than "human" row order).

To "force" row order, one needs to use "implied DO-loops," for example,

```
WRITE(6,101) ((A(I,J),J=1,4),I=1,3)
```

As with nested DO-loops, the nested implied DO-loops force the inner loop to be done completely (4 times) for each pass of the

74

outer loop (cf. section 5.7). Since the inner loop controls the second subscript, the effect is that the second subscript varies faster than the first subscript, thereby producing row order.

9.10 OVERUSE OF FORMATS WITH ARRAYS

As discussed earlier in Section 4.6, if there are more vairables than FORMAT field descriptors, then the FORMAT statement is re-used until all the variables are either READ into or WRITTEN out. This feature can be useful when dealing with arrays.

Let us look at the following example with arrays, similar to the example in Section 4.6.

```
      WRITE(6,102)  (A(I),B(I),I=1,10)
102   FORMAT(1X,2F20.5)
```

As in the previous example, FORMAT 102 only provides for two numeric fields. However, the WRITE statement has, in effect, 20 variables which it wants to write out. Therefore, FORMAT 102 gets re-used 10 times, each time starting a new line. However, if FORMAT 102 were changed to allow three numbers per line, the output would consist of seven lines, with three variables per line for the first six lines, and two variables on the last line. The order of the variables would be the same, i.e., A(1), then B(1), then A(2), then B(2), then A(3), then B(3), etc.

CHAPTER 10

SUBPROGRAMS

10.1 OVERVIEW

There are two types of subprograms in FORTRAN, SUB-ROUTINEs and FUNCTIONs. FORTRAN SUBROUTINEs correspond to what are called Procedures in some other languages. They are program subsections which can accept input parameters and change some of them. FORTRAN FUNCTIONs are similar to SUBROUTINEs with the major difference being that a FUNCTION also returns one specific value, a value which can be used, for example, in an arithmetic expression.

In FORTRAN (unlike some other contemporary languages), recursive calling by FUNCTIONs or SUBROUTINEs of themselves is not possible.

10.2 SUBROUTINES

To write the code for a subroutine, one uses a special SUB-ROUTINE header statement to begin the code (corresponding to a PROGRAM statement), and uses a RETURN statement as the last logical statement in the code (corresponding to the STOP statement in the main program). For example,

```
7+

SUBROUTINE name ( <formal parameter list> )

  .

  .

  .

RETURN
END
```

Notes:

a. RETURN is used in SUBROUTINEs and FUNCTIONs instead of STOP. It signifies the logical end of the subprogram. As with STOP, there can be more than one RETURN in a SUBROUTINE.

b. The parameter list, enclosed in parentheses after the SUBROUTINE name, contains only the variable names (separated by commas). The types and array dimensions are declared internally within the SUBROUTINE.

c. All variables are LOCAL and should be re-declared. There are no global variables in FORTRAN. Therefore, in particular, ARRAYS must be re-declared.

d. The code for SUBROUTINE comes after the main program code. If there is more than one SUBROUTINE, they are all placed together without any concern about order.

e. All statement numbers are also local, i.e., independent of numbers in the main program or any other subprogram.

f. In cases where the subprogram is totally self contained, for example, where it generates and/or prints information and neither receives nor gives information to the calling program, the parameter list (and the enclosing parentheses) is omitted.

To CALL a SUBROUTINE from the main program (or from any other subprogram), one uses the key word CALL, followed by the name of the SUBROUTINE, followed by actual parameters (separated by commas) enclosed in parentheses. For example,

```
7+
CALL name ( <actual parameter list> )
```

The actual arguments used in the CALL statement and the formal (or "dummy") parameters used in the definition statement must match in number, order, and type. Switching the order of the parameters, neglecting to declare the data type of any variables used as parameters, or omitting parameters can lead to errors. Sometimes the errors may be caught by the compiler before execution, but sometimes they are not, resulting in incorrect answers with hard to detect causes.

Note: If the SUBROUTINE has no formal parameter list (cf. note f above), then there is no actual parameter list (nor any parentheses) in the CALL statement.

10.3 SUBROUTINE EXAMPLE

As an example, let us consider the following SUBROUTINE which calculates the two roots of a polynomial, given its coefficients, by using the quadratic formula.

```
SUBROUTINE ROOTS(A,B,C,PROOT,NROOT)
REAL A,B,C,PROOT,NROOT,RAD
RAD=SQRT(B*B-4.0*A*C)
PROOT=(-B+RAD)/(2.0*A)
```

78

```
NROOT=(-B-RAD)/(2.0*A)
RETURN
END
```

This code would come after the main program in the code listing, and in the calling section, one might find something like the following:

```
...
READ(5,101)A,B,C
CALL ROOTS(A,B,C,X1,X2)
WRITE(6,102)X1,X2
...
```

Note: The formal parameters PROOT and NROOT may be termed "output only" parameters (since they convey no input information to the SUBROUTINE), and correspond to the actual parameters X1 and X2.

10.4 ARRAYS AS PARAMETERS

If a programmer wishes to pass an **entire** array, only the name of the array without any subscript is listed, both in the calling statement and in the code. However, the array must be declared as an array both in the calling program and the subprogram. For example, this program sums the values stored in an array of size 10.

```
PROGRAM MAIN
REAL B(10), TOTAL
...
CALL SUMARR(B,TOTAL)
```

```
          . . .
      END
C

      SUBROUTINE SUMARR(A,SUM)
      REAL A(10),SUM
      INTEGER I
      SUM = A(1)
      DO 10 I=2,10
          SUM=SUM+A(I)
10    CONTINUE
      RETURN
      END
```

It may happen that a programmer might want to use the same subprogram for arrays of different sizes. However, this can cause problems since many FORTRAN compilers demand that the formal (subprogram) and actual (calling program) arrays be dimensioned exactly the same, eliminating the possibility of the subprogram array corresponding to two different sized arrays in the calling program. To solve this dilemma, two general schemes are used.

In many implementations, it is permitted to dimension any ONE-dimensional array with the dimension one, e.g.

```
REAL A(1)
```

This is permitted since in FORTRAN, for a parameter which is an array, no new memory space is reserved, but a link is established with the variable in the calling program by passing its memory address. Since the subscripts used for the array are calculated inside the subprogram, the limit specified in the declaration is ultimately immaterial to the compiler. All the compiler needs is some sort of indicator that the variable in question is an array rather than a scalar.

However in some recent implementations, checks are performed for "subscripts out of range," so declaring an array with a dimension of one would cause problems. Therefore, as an alternate method for declaring arrays which are parameters, a variable upper limit is permitted in the declaration statement, i.e., one can write,

```
REAL A(N)
```

where both A and N are parameters passed into the subprogram. **Note:** This type of indefinite dimensioning is only allowed in SUBPROGRAMS, and only for arrays which are PARAMETERS!!

For two and higher dimensional arrays, if the first method is used, the last subscript may be one, but all the other subscripts must be the same in the subprogram, as they were in the calling program. If the second method is used, all the subscripts may be variables, but all these variables must be parameters passed from the calling program.

As an example of using the second method, the following subroutine calculates the average of the numbers stored in an array.

```
SUBROUTINE AVER(ARR,N,AVE)
REAL ARR(N), AVE,SUM
INTEGER N,I
SUM=ARR(1)
DO 10 I=2,N
   SUM=SUM + ARR(I)
```

```
10 CONTINUE
   AVE=SUM/N
   RETURN
   END
```

And in the calling program, one might have,

```
CALL AVER(GRADE,25,AVERAG)
```

and elsewhere GRADE would be declared as follows:

```
REAL GRADE(25)
```

10.5 FORTRAN USER-DEFINED FUNCTIONS

In theory, FORTRAN user-defined FUNCTIONS are similar to FORTRAN library functions and to user-defined functions in other languages. To write code for a user FUNCTION, one follows the same rules as for a SUBROUTINE but substitutes the word FUNCTION for SUBROUTINE. The key word FUNCTION may be preceded by a TYPE name if one wishes to supersede the default variable typing or if one simply wishes to be explicit.

For example,

```
7+
<optional type> FUNCTION name ( <formal
   variable list> )
. . .
RETURN
END
```

Notes:

a. In general, all the rules mentioned above for FORTRAN SUBROUTINES also apply to FORTRAN FUNCTIONs.

b. Within the FUNCTION, the FUNCTION **name** is a local variable. Since the general rules for FUNCTIONs are such that they actually take on a value, the name (as a variable) must be given a value somewhere within the code for the function.

c. As mentioned above, FORTRAN FUNCTIONs are *not* recursive, so the FUNCTION name should never appear on the right side of any assignment.

One could rewrite part of the above SUBROUTINE as a FORTRAN FUNCTION as follows:

```
7+
REAL FUNCTION PROOT(A,B,C)
REAL A,B,C
PROOT =  (-B+SQRT(B*B-4.0*A*C))/(2.0*A)
RETURN
END
```

Then, in the calling section, one would just use the function (similar to the way the library functions such as SQRT are used within an arithmetic statement), for example,

```
. . .
READ(5,101)A,B,C
X1=2.0*PROOT(A,B,C)
. . .
```

83

Note: Since a FUNCTION takes on a specific value, it must be of a specific type. That type may be explicitly listed in the subprogram definition code, but the FUNCTION type also plays an important rule in the calling section. Thus, in any segment of code (main PROGRAM, SUBROUTINE, FUNCTION) which uses ("calls") a user-defined FUNCTION, the FUNCTION name should also be declared as a local variable in a standard type statement to avoid any type-mismatch errors. For example, in the section which uses the FUNCTION PROOT given above, there should be a declaration statement,

```
7+
REAL PROOT, A, B, C
```

10.6 PARAMETER PASSING IN FORTRAN

When the major computer languages are analyzed, four principal methods to communicate via (or to "pass") parameters between a calling program and a subprogram can be identified. The standard names for these methods are:

call by value
call by reference (or "address")
call by name (or "expression")
call by result (or "value-result")

In some languages (e.g., Pascal, Ada), the programmer has the choice of determining the passing scheme for each parameter.

In other languages (e.g., FORTRAN, C), the user has no choice. The passing scheme is predetermined, but sometimes it is different for arrays than for scalars.

In FORTRAN, the specific passing methods are predetermined by the implementation, and no choice by the user is possible. In FORTRAN, the actual parameters are changed in the calling segment, if the formal parameters were changed in the subprogram segment. However, the methods used to produce the change in value may vary from implementation to implementation.

Most implementations of FORTRAN-IV use

call by result (value-result) for simple (scalar) variables and

call by reference (address) for arrays.

Most implementations of FORTRAN-77 use

call by reference for ALL parameters (scalars or arrays).

In CALL BY RESULT (VALUE-RESULT), the subprogram copies VALUES from the actual parameters in the calling program. However, it has independent memory locations in the subprogram and these values may be changed independently of the variables originally associated with them in the calling program. When the subprogram is finished (i.e., when the RETURN statement is reached), the associated variables in the calling program are changed.

In CALL BY REFERENCE (ADDRESS), no new memory locations are allocated. Instead, a link is set up so that whenever a subprogram variable is referenced, the corresponding variable in the calling program is accessed and changed.

Note that in both of these calling conventions, the variables can be changed upon completion of the subprogram. This is not true of the call-by-value parameters (used in Pascal and C). In CALL-BY-VALUE, the subprogram sets up new independent memory locations, copies the values from the actual parameters (as in call-by-value-result), but does *not* change any variables in the calling program upon its completion.

To show that problems may occur if a programmer is unclear as to which parameter passing scheme is used, and thus, to exactly what is happening between the main program and the subroutine, let us examine the following example, written in a psuedo-language.

```
function icrazy(i,j,k):integer
i=j+k
j=j+k
icrazy=i+j+k
k=j
return
end
```

Suppose the main program code included the following:

```
n = 5
ivalue = icrazy(n,n,n)
ivalue = ivalue + n
write (ivalue)
```

Then, depending on the type of "calling" used, one gets three different answers!!

```
CALL BY VALUE-RESULT (FORTRAN-IV SCALAR)
     = 35
CALL BY VALUE (cf. PASCAL and C)
     = 30
CALL BY ADDRESS (FORTRAN ARRAYS, FORTRAN-77 SCALAR)
     = 80
```

In the CALL BY VALUE, the *n* in the calling code remains unchanged, whereas in the CALL BY VALUE-RESULT it changes. In the CALL BY ADDRESS, the one memory location identified by *n* in the main program has three additional names in the function, *i*, *j*, and *k*. Therefore whenever any one of them changes, the other three change values as well!

10.7 ONE STATEMENT FUNCTIONS

It is also possible to define a one-line function at the beginning of each program segment in FORTRAN. After the type declaration statements and other initial statements, and before the first executable statement, one defines a statement in one line, similar to the typical mathematical statement definition. For example,

```
F(X) = X*X
```

or

```
G(X) = 2.0*X**3 + 3.0*X*X + 4.0*X - 2.5
```

Then, in the code, one uses these functions as any other functions. For example,

```
. . .
A = F(2) - 3.0*G(3)
FPX=(F(X+DELTAX)-F(X))/DELTAX
. . .
```

10.8 EXTERNAL AND INTRINSIC STATEMENTS

Occasionally, one may want to use the same subprogram code with a number of different functions (either library or user-defined). In these situations it would be useful if one could pass a function name as a parameter to the subprogram. This is permitted in FORTRAN if one lists the various functions which will be passed as arguments in an EXTERNAL or an INTRINSIC statement in the CALLING segment. One uses EXTERNAL if the function is user-defined. In FORTRAN-77, one uses INTRINSIC if the function is part of the FORTRAN library functions (FORTRAN-IV does not have this statement). These specification statements come with the other specification statements, before the first executable statement in the calling segment.

For example,

```
7+
EXTERNAL F1,F2,F3
INTRINSIC SIN,COS
 . . .
CALL MYSUB1(SIN,X,Y,OUT1)
CALL MYSUB1(COS,X,Y,OUT2)
CALL MYSUB2(F2,Y)
CALL MYSUB2(F3,Z)
 . . .
```

In a subprogram (SUBROUTINE or FUNCTION), one must use an EXTERNAL statement again listing the function arguments which have been passed if one wishes to pass these same arguments again (and they cannot otherwise be identified as subprograms).

For example, suppose F and SUB1 are intended to be dummy names for subprograms to be passed into SUB2.

```
+7
SUBROUTINE SUB2(A,B,F,SUB1)
```

```
EXTERNAL F
CALL SUB1(F,A,B)
RETURN
END
```

Since SUB1 was used in the CALL statement, the compiler recognizes it as a SUBROUTINE and it need not be listed in the EXTERNAL statement. However, since there is no indication that F is a subprogram (by default typing, it is a REAL variable), it must be listed in the EXTERNAL statement.

Note: In FORTRAN-77, one cannot pass as arguments generic function names, type conversion functions, lexical comparison functions, or maximum and minimum functions. In FORTRAN-IV, one can only pass those function names specifically designated as external (cf. Chapter 6, Section 6.2).

10.9 MULTIPLE ENTRY POINTS (FORTRAN-77)

If one is using FORTRAN-77, one can combine several similar SUBROUTINEs or FUNCTIONs into one larger subprogram, yet retain independent ENTRY points into the subprogram code by using the ENTRY subheader statement. The ENTRY statement is similar to a FUNCTION or SUBROUTINE in that the entry point is given a name and an argument list. Thus, for example,

```
7+
ENTRY NEWSRT(A,B)
```

The entry name (e.g., NEWSRT) for a FUNCTION should be declared as to its correct type after the header statement of the subprogram, along with any parameters in the parameter list.

89

The ENTRY statement provides an alternate place to start the action of the subprogram. This can be useful especially if two or more subprograms share a significant amount of common code.

10.10 SAVE STATEMENT (FORTRAN-77)

Normally when a subprogram is completed, the values of all variables are left undefined. If one wishes to re-use a FUNCTION or SUBROUTINE several times and also wishes the previous local variables to retain old values, this can be done by means of invoking the SAVE specification statement of FORTRAN-77.

The SAVE statement comes before any DATA or executable statement and lists those variables whose values are to be SAVEd. The name of a COMMON block may also be listed. If no variables are listed, all variable values are saved. As an example, if one wishes to SAVE the values of variables A, B, and C, the following statement is used:

```
7+
SAVE A, B, C
```

CHAPTER 11

CHARACTER VARIABLES

11.1 DECLARING CHARACTER VARIABLES

In earlier versions of FORTRAN (FORTRAN-IV), character information was usually stored in INTEGER variables. Even now, convention demands that older programs written this way run on FORTRAN-77 compilers as well. Usually such programs only need minor changes, depending on how many characters could be stored in one integer variable.

However, in FORTRAN-77, CHARACTER is a standard type for variables. The general character type declaration statement is similar to other FORTRAN type declaration statements.

```
7+
CHARACTER <variable list>
```

or

```
7+
CHARACTER*n <variable list>
```

or a combination.

In the second example, the *n* refers to the number of characters which the programmer wishes to store in one variable. This *n designation can also be appended to any variable in the variable list. If the *n is omitted from the word CHARACTER, the compiler assumes one character per variable. However, if *n is appended to variables, the local number supersedes any number appended to the word CHARACTER.

For example, suppose we have the following declarations:

```
CHARACTER*20 NAME
CHARACTER*3 PETE, SAM*5, FRED
CHARACTER MSG1*2,MSG2*4,MSG3*10,MSG4
```

then this would declare that

	NAME could store	20 characters
	PETE could store	3 characters
	FRED could store	3 characters
	SAM could store	5 characters
	MSG1 could store	2 characters
	MSG2 could store	4 characters
	MSG3 could store	10 characters
and	MSG4 could store only	1 character.

11.2 ASSIGNMENTS

To assign "constant" values (i.e. a string of characters) to a character variable, one surrounds the string with single quotes, e.g.,

```
PETE = 'SAM'
SAM = 'PATTY'
```

11.3 INPUT/OUTPUT

To READ values from outside the program into a character variable (or in FORTRAN-IV, into an integer variable), or to output a character value using a WRITE statement, one uses the A field descriptor in a FORMAT statement. For example,

```
        PETE = 'SAM'
        SAM = 'DENIS'
        WRITE(6,10) PETE, SAM
10      FORMAT(1x,A3,2X,A5)
```

or

```
        CHARACTER*5 A,B
        READ(5,101) A,B
101     FORMAT(2A5)
        WRITE(6,102) B,A
102     FORMAT(1X,2A5)
        STOP
        END
```

Suppose the second example had an input of

```
1 2 3 4 5 6 7 8 9 10
N O W   I S   T H E
```

the output would be

```
cc 1 2 3 4 5 6 7 8 9 10
   S   T H E N O W   I
```

If one uses free-format input, the character string should be

93

enclosed in single quotes, but quotes should *not* be used with FORMATTED input. With free-format input, the input subroutines must determine which type the input data is, so it needs a signal, the quote, to indicate that the data is character. However, with FORMAT statements, the field descriptor determines both the columns in which the data is to be found and also the type of the data, so such additional signals are not needed.

11.4 ASSIGNMENTS OF DIFFERENT LENGTH

When using character variables and strings of different length in assignment statements, the intuitive rules normally hold, namely:

1. If a longer string is assigned to a shorter length variable, the end of the string is truncated;

2. If a small string is assigned to a longer length variable, the end of the string is padded with blanks.

For example,

```
      CHARACTER A*2,B*3,C*4
      B = 'SAM'
      A = B
      C = B
      WRITE(6,103) A,C
103   FORMAT(1X,A2,2X,A4)
      STOP
      END
```

```
Output
cc 1 2 3 4 5 6 7 8 9 10
   S A     S A M
```

94

When A gets B's value, the final M in SAM is truncated since A can only store two characters. When C gets the value of B, C is padded with another character, a blank, at the end, since C can store 4 characters, and B only has 3.

11.5 CONCATENATION OPERATOR

FORTRAN-77 also provides a way of joining two strings together by what is called the concatenation operator and is indicated by two slash signs together, //. This unites two separate strings into one. For example,

```
      CHARACTER NAME1*3,NAME2*4,NAME3*7
      NAME1 = 'PAT'
      NAME2 = 'RICK'
      NAME3 = NAME1//NAME2
      WRITE(6,23) NAME3
23    FORMAT(1X,A7)
      STOP
      END
```

would have the following output

```
cc 1 2 3 4 5 6 7 8 9 10
   P A T R I C K
```

Concatenation's precedence is below that of the arithmetic operators and above that of the logical operators.

11.6 OTHER CHARACTER OPERATIONS: FUNCTIONS FOR CHARACTER DATA

FORTRAN-77 also provides other ways of working with character data. The following FUNCTIONs can be useful

ICHAR(C)	Gives the INTEGER equivalent of the single character in the variable C (usually the ASCII code).
CHAR(I)	Gives the CHARACTER equivalent of the integer I (this is the inverse function of ICHAR).
LEN(C)	Gives the INTEGER length of C.
INDEX(C1,C2)	If the sub-string C2 is completely contained in the string C1, this will return the INTEGER which indicates the starting position of C2 within C1.

11.7 COMPARING CHARACTER DATA

It is possible to compare two character strings, since the comparison is made based on the numeric code of the characters, and the code follows alphabetical order. Thus, if one things of alphabetical order as a different version of numeric order, then the logical relational operators can be used with the expected results, e.g., 'A' .LE.' C' is .TRUE. and 'Z' .GT. 'P' is also .TRUE. since less than and greater than in the alphabetical context refers to being earlier or later in the normal ordered list (this is similar to the meaning of these operators with numbers).

In addition, FORTRAN-77 also provides several CHARACTER comparison functions which perform the same comparison functions (as the logical relational operators) and return LOGICAL values as outputs.

LGE(C1,C2)	"Lexically Greater than or Equal to" – this function compares the two strings stored in C1 and C2, and determines whether C1 equals C2 or whether C1 follows C2 in the lexical se-

quence (i.e., alphabetical order, or the collating sequence). If so, it returns the LOGICAL value .TRUE., else it returns .FALSE.

LGT(C1,C2)   "Lexically Greater Than".

LLE(C1,C2)   "Lexically Less than or Equal to".

LLT(C1,C2)   "Lexically Less Than".

These functions are used in the same way as LGE with similar output values.

One must be careful that one does not confuse the "human" meaning and "human" implied order of character strings with the actual computer (alphabetical) order. Take the following example:

```
CHARACTER*3 A,B,C
A = 'TWO'
B = 'TEN'
C = 'SIX'
```

Then, we have

```
A .GE. B is .TRUE.
```

and

```
C .LE. B is .TRUE.
```

Even though 2 is less than 10, as far as the dictionary is concerned, the word 'two' comes after the word 'ten' and thus 'two' > 'ten'.

Different implementations use different coding systems, so even though all the capital letters follow the established order, and all the small letters follow the established order, there are no standard rules for whether small letters come before capital letters and where numbers and special characters fit into the schema. When using the character functions LGE, LGT, LLE, LLT, the ASCII sequence is always followed even on a non-ASCII machine. However, when using the logical relational operators, the coding system of the implementation is used.

11.8 SUBSTRINGS

One can also specify substrings in FORTRAN-77 by using notation similar to array notation. For example, if A can store 10 characters, to indicate the substring consisting of characters 4 through 8, we write A(4:8). If one omits the first or last number, the compiler will assume the first or last character in the complete string. This notation can be used anywhere and on either side of assignment statements, and combined with the concatenation operator.

For example,

```
CHARACTER*24 B,C
B = 'A SMALL STEP FOR A MAN'
C = B(3:3)//B(:1)//B(4:4)
B(18:) = C
PRINT *,B
STOP
END
```

This program assigns to C the value of 'SAM' (the third, first and fourth characters of B), and then replaces the eighteenth through last characters of B with C, i.e., B now becomes 'A SMALL STEP

FOR SAM'.

The only restriction is that it is not permitted to duplicate character positions on both sides of the assignment statement. For example,

```
A(4:6)  =  A(2:4)
```

is illegal since the fourth character position appears on both sides!

CHAPTER 12

DOUBLE PRECISION AND COMPLEX NUMBERS

12.1 DOUBLE PRECISION VARIABLES AND CONSTANTS

DOUBLE PRECISION real arithmetic usually at least doubles the number of digits accuracy. To declare variables as DOUBLE PRECISION, one must use an explicit type variable declaration statement with the key words DOUBLE PRECISION, i.e.

```
7+
DOUBLE PRECISION A,B,C
```

There is no default typing for double precision. In input and output, one can use a D field descriptor in the FORMAT statements – the rules are the same as for the E descriptors.

For constants, one always uses scientific (exponential) form substituting a D for the E. Since 10 to the power of 0 is 1, one can always express a double precision number as a simple fixed point number followed by D00. In other words, zero as a double precision number is 0.0D00. 300 can be written 3.0D02 and pi can be written 3.1415926D00.

A few systems use the notation REAL*16 as an alternative to (or even in place of) the standard terminology of DOUBLE PRECISION.

12.2 COMPLEX VARIABLES AND CONSTANTS

To declare certain variables as COMPLEX, one must once again use an explicit declaration statement, e.g.,

```
7+
COMPLEX C
```

COMPLEX numbers are stored as two adjacent real numbers, so all input and output is done via two E or F descriptors.

To indicate a COMPLEX constant, one uses parentheses around the two component numbers separated by a comma. For example, to indicate $a = 3 + 4i$, one writes

```
A = (3,4)
```

in FORTRAN.

12.3 CONVERSION FUNCTIONS

Conversion functions exist for all purposes (cf. Chapter 6). For example, to convert from real to complex, one uses the library function CMPLX, e.g.,

```
C = CMPLX(A,B)
```

where A and B are real variables or numbers.

101

To extract the real or imaginary part of a complex number, one uses the library functions REAL or AIMAG, e.g.,

```
A = REAL (C)
```

or

```
B = AIMAG (C)
```

To calculate the conjugate of a complex number $c = a + bi$ (i.e., to find $a - bi$), one uses the library function CONJG, e.g.,

```
CBAR = CONJG (C)
```

CHAPTER 13

ADDITIONAL SPECIFICATION STATEMENTS

13.1 DATA STATEMENTS

A DATA statement is used to initialize variables with values. In one sense it is misnamed, since its purpose is initialization. It normally appears before any executable statement (after the other declarations statements) and is executed once (even if it appears in a subprogram which is called often). In the DATA statement, one lists the variables to be initialized followed by the initial value enclosed in slash bars. Several variables (and values) are separated by commas. Arrays are listed without any subscript if the entire array is to be initialized. For example,

```
7+
DATA A/1.0/,I/2/
```

or

```
REAL B(5)
DATA B/1.0,2.0,3.0,4.0,5.0/
```

or

```
DATA I,J,K/3*0/
```

The second example shows that the same process can take place for arrays in DATA statements as happens in a READ or WRITE statement – if no subscript is given, FORTRAN "expands" the array named to include all the elements of the array. Thus, since there are five elements in the array B, five values must be given within the slash lines. The third example shows that it is possible to "multiply" a value within the slash lines – saving time and energy in explicitly listing values, especially if all the values are the same.

13.2 COMMON

A COMMON statement is one way of designating certain variables to be stored in a COMMON section of memory and shared by different program segments. It thus becomes a way of approximating in FORTRAN the concept of global variables of other languages. However, no variable in FORTRAN is "global" automatically – to approximate this concept, the COMMON statement must be used. Practically, it becomes a way of avoiding listing variables as parameters when using subprograms.

The key word COMMON is followed by the names of variables one wishes to be held in COMMON (separated by commas). This must be done in each subprogram which is to use these variables.

For example,

```
7+
COMMON A,B,C
```

Notes:

a. The variables listed should already be declared (as scalars or arrays) in type declaration statements which precede the COMMON statements.

b. Order is all-important. Names mean nothing. In this sense the COMMON statement is very similar to the way the parameter list works between the calling segment and the subprogram code – the first names are associated with each other, then the second names, and so on. For example, if, in the main program you had

```
COMMON A,B,C
```

and in the subroutine you had

```
COMMON B,C,A
```

then, what was called A in the main program would be called B in the subroutine and so on.

c. You must include a COMMON statement in each subprogram which needs to use the variables listed. Moreover, each variable listed in a COMMON must be declared the same way in each subprogram where it is found. If certain variables are declared as arrays in one segment, they must also be declared as arrays everywhere, even if they are never used in a given subprogram.

The COMMON reserves memory space and names it according to the names given in the particular subprogram. Thus the same memory location may have more than one name. No check is made for consistency. It is possible to turn many arrays into one array as long as the number of total memory locations are more or less the same. For example, one might have in the main program,

```
REAL A(10),B(10),C(10)
COMMON A,B,C
```

and in a subroutine

```
REAL D(30)
COMMON D
```

In this case, what is called A(7) in the main program is D(7) in the subroutine, but what is B(4) in the main program is D(14) in the subroutine (since both are the fourteenth item in each list).

One can also name the COMMON area, allowing the possibility of having more than one COMMON area. One such named COMMON area might be used between the main program and one subroutine and another between the main program and a different subroutine. To give a COMMON area a name, one encloses the chosen name between slashes after the word COMMON. For example,

```
COMMON /EXAM/ A,B,C
COMMON /GRADE/ G,F,H
```

Variables may appear in only one named COMMON block.

If one is using CHARACTER variables and wishes to place them in COMMON, one should use named COMMON areas and keep all CHARACTER variables in one area and numeric variables in another. Mixing CHARACTER and numeric types in a COMMON statement on most systems leads to errors.

13.3 INITIALIZING COMMON VARIABLES— BLOCK DATA SUBPROGRAMS

Variables in a named COMMON block may be initialized only by means of a BLOCK DATA subprogram. This subprogram only contains the variables to be initialized and a DATA statement for the initialization. A name for the BLOCK DATA unit is optional. For example,

```
7+
BLOCK DATA INIT1
REAL GRADES(20)
COMMON /SECT1/GRADES
DATA GRADES/20*1.0/
END
```

Notes:

a. A RETURN statement is not used.

b. Named COMMON blocks must be fully specified, even when only some of its entries are initialized.

13.4 EQUIVALENCE

This statement is used to give two names to the same memory location in the same program segment. The general form is

```
7+
EQUIVALENCE(A,B),  (C,D)
```

This statement will make A and B equivalent names for the same memory location, and C and D for another memory location.

It is also permitted to equivalence arrays, even of different sizes, by equivalencing the "starting" elements in two arrays. For example,

```
REAL A(10),B(5)
EQUIVALENCE  (A(3),B(1))
```

This will make A(3) and B(1) equivalent names for the same memory location, and also A(4) and B(2), and A(5) and B(3), and A(6) and B(4), and finally A(7) and B(5).

The EQUIVALENCE statement was of more usefulness when most programming was done via cards, and it could happen that one programmer used one variable name and another programmer used a different variable name for the same concept. Instead of retyping a great number of cards, two different names were made equivalent via this statement.

However, with text editors and terminals, this problem is less likely to occur. Nevertheless, the EQUIVALENCE statement can occasionally be useful to simplify code, sometimes making it more efficient. Take the case of trying to zero a multi-dimensional array in the middle of a program. One can make a one-dimensional array equivalent to a multi-dimensional array, and then write code to zero the one-dimensional array, code which will be much simpler than the other code. For example, suppose we had

```
REAL A(4,4,4),A2(64)
EQUIVALENCE (A(1,1,1),A2(1))
```

then instead of writing

```
      DO 20 J1=1,4
        DO 30 J2=1,4
          DO 40 J3=1,4
            A(J1,J2,J3)=0.0
40        CONTINUE
30    CONTINUE
20 CONTINUE
```

one can write

```
      DO 20 J=1,64
         A2(J)=0.0
   20 CONTINUE
```

13.5 PARAMETER (FORTRAN-77)

The FORTRAN-77 PARAMETER statement is used to turn an identifier into a constant. After the key word PARAMETER, one assigns a value to a parameter name (with an equals sign) and encloses this in parentheses. The PARAMETER names should be declared in a type statement prior to the PARAMETER statement, so that each identifier matches in type the value received. More than one assignment can be included in the set of parentheses, if separated by commas. For example,

```
   7+
   PARAMETER  (PI=3.1415926,E=2.718281826)
```

Arithmetic expressions may also be used in calculating values for the parameter.

```
   PARAMETER(HALFPI=3.1415926/2.0,THIRD=1.0/3.0)
```

Parameters defined in a PARAMETER statement cannot be used as variables. Attempting to change the value of these parameters will result in errors.

13.6 ORDER OF SPECIFICATION STATEMENTS

All the specification statements normally come together at the beginning of a program segment, but they have a relative order. The following is the preferred order.

[PROGRAM, FUNCTION, SUBROUTINE, or BLOCK DATA header line]
IMPLICIT type
PARAMETER
type (INTEGER, REAL, LOGICAL, CHARACTER,
      DOUBLE PRECISION - in any order)
DIMENSION
COMMON
EQUIVALENCE
DATA
one-line function designators
[executable statements]
[END]

Notes:

a. COMMENTS may come anywhere before the END (including before and after the header).

b. FORMAT and ENTRY statements may appear anywhere between the header and the END.

c. DATA statements may actually appear anywhere between the IMPLICIT statements and the END, but the variables listed are only initialized once.

d. PARAMETER statements may actually appear anywhere between the header and the one-line function designators. However, parameters must be defined before use in other specification statements, and the identifiers should be declared as to correct type before receiving a value.

Comment lines	PROGRAM, FUNCTION, SUBROUTINE, or BLOCK DATA statements		
	FORMAT and ENTRY statements	PARAMETER statements	IMPLICIT statements
			other specification statements
		DATA statements	statement function statements
			executable statements
	END statement		

CHAPTER 14

LESS FREQUENTLY USED AND NON-STANDARD FEATURES

14.1 PAUSE STATEMENT

The PAUSE statement causes the program to temporarily halt. An optional number may follow the keyword. To restart the program, the FORTRAN manual for the version you are using should be consulted.

For example,

```
7+
PAUSE 234
```

will cause the program to temporarily halt and the number 234 to appear on the terminal.

14.2 ASSIGN STATEMENT

The ASSIGN statement is used to assign a value to an integer variable, but the value assigned must correspond to a statement label in use in that program segment. For example,

```
7+
ASSIGN 352 TO LABEL1
```

will give LABEL1 the value of 352, where 352 should correspond to a statement label in the program segment. The ASSIGN is frequently used with the assigned GO TO, but also may be used to enable a READ or WRITE statement to use a variable in lieu of a constant for the FORMAT statement number.

14.3 ASSIGNED GO TO STATEMENT

The assigned GO TO statement enables a transfer to take place based on the present value of an integer variable whose value was assigned by means of an ASSIGN statement. For example,

```
7+
GO TO LABEL1
```

would transfer control to the statement label which was most recently ASSIGNed to LABEL1.

Optionally, a list of permitted statement labels enclosed in parentheses may follow the variable identifier (preceded by an optional comma). For example,

```
7+
GO TO LABEL1, (10,20,252,999)
```

indicates that the possible values of LABEL1 are only the four listed. If LABEL1 does not have any of those values, an error occurs.

14.4 WHILE LOOPS

Although the WHILE loop is not part of standard FORTRAN-77, many compilers include it. It simulates the WHILE loop found in other languages, but may have slightly different syntax. For example, WATFIV-S uses

```
WHILE (A.LE.B) DO
    ...
END WHILE
```

while other versions are

```
DO WHILE (A.LE.B)
    ...
END DO
```

14.5 COMMENTS AT END OF LINES

Some FORTRAN versions allow the use of comments after the executable part of a statement by placing an exclamation point (!) in the line.

14.6 MULTIPLE STATEMENT LINES

Some FORTRAN versions allow the inclusion of more than one statement on a line, separated by semicolons.

14.7 MULTIPLE ASSIGNMENTS

Some FORTRAN versions allow multiple assignments, for example,

```
A = B = C = 0.0
```

CHAPTER 15

COMPARISON BETWEEN FORTRAN AND PASCAL

FORTRAN	PASCAL
4 fields per line, continuation lines.	"free"-format lines.
Variable names are no longer than 6 characters.	Variable names can be any length, but only the first 8 (standard) are examined for uniqueness.
Variables need not be declared.	Variables must be declared.
6 variable types: integer, real, character*n, logical, double precision, complex (new types cannot be created).	4 variable types: integer, real, char, boolean (new types can be defined)
Variables are local to the segment used, unless one uses a COMMON.	Variables can be global.
Assignment is =	Assignment is :=
Exponentiation operator **	No exponentiation

FORTRAN	PASCAL
/ is both integer and real division.	/ is real, DIV is integer.
DO-loop (F-66 low index >= 1, can only count up – F-77 indices can be <0, step can be negative.)	FOR-loop "to" counts up, "downto" counts down, step size is always one.
"SUBROUTINE"	"PROCEDURE"
Subprogram code comes after END of main program.	Subprogram code comes before BEGIN of main progam.
Subprograms are *not* recursive.	Subprograms can be recursive.
Parameters are passed via address or value-result (FORTRAN-66 scalars).	Parameters are passed via address (VAR) or value ("value").
I/O very developed. (carriage control characters)	I/O relatively un-developed.
Some versions have version of WHILE loop.	WHILE, REPEAT loops exist.
"computed" GO TO	(approximated by) CASE
ARRAYS use parentheses () Storage order is by COLUMN.	ARRAYS use square brackets []. Storage order is by ROW.
PARAMETER, DATA	(approximated by) CONST
No semicolons, BEGINS.	—

INDEX